Everybody On Stage For The Hawaiian Number

Everybody On Stage For The Hawaiian Number

BRYAN MURPHY

StoryTerrace

CONTENTS

DEDICATION

This book is for my mommy. There are not enough pages to say what needs to be said. So, suffice it to say, this book is dedicated to my mom, who drilled it into my brain that "I could".

And to Roger – my honey, the cutie, the hubby, my pretty blue eyes, my "*doctor*" who diagnosed my dyscalculia (number dyslexia), who always remembered my type of arthritis, my dreamboat, my walking metric system converter – my everything.

THANK YOU

And for all those people who were nice and kind and helpful to me throughout my life. I thank you.

To those who were not sweet and lovely to me, pick a finger.

In fact, pick two. I have five.

(Hey, remember – I *AM* FROM BROOKLYN!)

Oh, and to the poor person who gets to edit this, I'm saying thank you and sorry NOW.

PROLOGUE

Ok. Over the years, some people have said I should write a book about my life. Why? It's my life and just me. This lockdown finally convinced me it might be fun, especially since I had the time. I certainly had nothing to do all day. Even my AI, Alexa was rude if I asked her what day it was: "Why? Do you have a date? Somewhere to go? So why do you want to know what day it is?" Perhaps, I decided, it would give me something to do, besides crying about not traveling and eating way too much.

One of the things I promised myself: I would not use this forum to get even or bad-mouth anyone (I really want to, though). But sorry, y'all, I'm hoping to stick to that. If I have to say something not very nice about anyone, I'm not going to mention names, just the incidents. I am aware there are a couple of "friends" on the outer circle of my life whose animus and envy are eating them alive, but that is their problem. Plus, I know there are a few folks who want me to talk about my so-called salacious love life. Nope. Not doing that, either ("Awwwwwwwww!" I hear you say).

By the by, I am bi-lingual. I speak and write both English and American. Consequently, throughout the book, you will see me go back and forth between the two languages. And now you know.

I have no idea where or when I first heard "***EVERYBODY ON STAGE FOR THE HAWAIIAN NUMBER,***" but it is from the 1965 film, *A Thousand Clowns* by Herb Gardner. Sometimes, when I was about to go on stage, I'd say it to whomever was around.

I wanted a fun title for the book. This popped into my head. Then, a brainstorm arose. Use the photo of me dressed as a pharaoh. Now *that* is fun.

The photo is from a show I did in school. I want that stomach back. Sigh. That is the closest I ever got to a six-pack, or any-number-pack tummy. This was during the 20 minutes in my life I was thin. I was so skinny, I walked at a 45-degree angle. My hips would enter a room five minutes before the rest of me. A relative once yelled at my mother to "Feed that child!"

Ahh, those were the days.

As I looked back over my cute little life, I suppose that, if not interesting, it certainly has been fun. So, join me now.

LADIES AND GENTLEMEN, PLACES PLEASE!

BRYAN MURPHY
IN
EVERYBODY ON STAGE
FOR THE HAWAIIAN NUMBER

STARRING

MOM, ROGER, KATHY

CO-STARRING

GLENN, THOM, THE DIVINE ONE, SARAH, ALEX, PARIS, DAN, ERNIE, GEORGE, BOBBY, THE ISRAELI SINGER, SHELDON, PENNY, RAJ, LONDON VICAR, NORBERTO, HONEY WEST, MARIA, GRETL, LIESL, FRIEDRICH, LOUISA, KURT, BRIGITTA, MARTA, FAMOUS '60S SINGER, DAWN HAMPTON, THE LADY CHABLIS, JACKIE ROBINSON, EVE ARDEN, BROADWAY STAR, MOIRA, JOHNNY, PATRICK, DAVID, MADAME LEONTYNE PRICE, TWA, NICK, NICK, PHIL, MR. D. LYNN, HERCULE, CEIL & HARRIET, SOL & HARV, MY KID AND HIS WIFE, MS. BAILEY, MISS MARPLE, AVIS, DINO, BIG TONY INFORMANT, IMA SUMAC, DR. DAVID, DUNKIN' DONUTS, RONNIE, UNCLE SAM, SONNY, MS. TURNER, THAT NEW YORK BASEBALL PLAYER, THE OTHER FAMOUS SINGER WHO MADE GOO-GOO EYES AT ME IN THE AIRPORT LOUNGE, AND, OF COURSE – LASSIE.

CURTAIN UP

ACT I

IT'S ME. IT'S BRYAN.

'm **Bryan Murphy**. I love my name. Murphy is cool, and more on that later, but BRYAN… I LOVE THAT NAME! BRYAN. Don't know what it is, but I love BRYAN.

I know, in the past, I asked my mom the reasons for my names. I do not recall what she said. I do recall she wanted to make sure my name could not be shortened; for example, Robert to Bob, Martin to Marty etc. She always wanted me and my brother, Glenn, to be called by our names. And don't you know, there were a few who did shorten it: Bryan to *Bry,* and one even went so far as to call me "*B*"! One of the ones who called me BRY could have called me anything and I would have responded.

As for my middle name, Willard – I hate it. It's annoying. Stupid. Dumb. Willard makes no sense to me. WILLARD! Really? And if I didn't hate it before, once I got to the UK and heard how they put the emphasis on it... Will-**ARD**, I really hated it. I never use it. Not even the W. The only time you'll see or hear me say that name is if it has something to do with the F.B.I. or C.I.A. or Interpol, or MI5. (Aww, come on, we all know there is no such thing as MI6. Even the people who work for MI6 know it doesn't exist).

Murphy. Ah, yeah. Having the name Murphy and throwing in the Bryan has caused confusion at times for some folk, and lots of fun for me. For, you see, the names do not match their perception of my face. I can be waiting to meet someone, and they call out my name and look through, past and around me. Then I stand up, and I see their confused countenance. I silently laugh to myself.

I have always trusted and believed my mother, so I'm going to give her this one. One time, I was going through her scrap books looking at the various cards, congrats on the birth of your son, and letters. One of the cards said something about "Congratulations on the birth of your son, BERNARD."

BERNARD???? BERNARD!

"Who is this Bernard kid with my place of birth and date? And what is his congratulations card doing in *your* scrap book, mom? Were you going to name me BERNARD???"

She said no. Her friend had made a mistake. You ain't kidding. A huge mistake. I can hear it now. "Oh, Bernie? Hey, Bern. Yo, Bernardie!"

Lucky she got my vote of trust. I don't know how old a

baby is when he starts to crawl, but I would have made the *Guinness Book of Records*. I would have been the first baby crawling into the family court on his own, to charge my mother with cruelty and child abuse for calling me Bernard. Then I would crawl my way to Civil Court, to have my name changed. If I can't be Bryan, I like Marc, but it must have the "C". Or Richard. Not Dickie or Ricky or Rich. Richard!

Now, mind you, I have absolutely nothing against Willard or Bernard for other men. Just not me. I am, and will always remain, BRYAN MURPHY. Or just Bryan, if you will.

Would you believe, when I was working, I'd send my photos – that have my name at the bottom – to clubs. They do advertising with the photo and still spell my name incorrectly at times. I've been BRIAN, BRAIN, BYRON, BRYEN. And it's right there in front of them!

I'd always wanted a logo when I started working. When I was doing volunteer work at the Gay Switchboard in New York, one of my fellow volunteers was a guy named Neal Pozner, who was a graphic artist. Famous, too. He did the artwork for Sondheim's CD for *Assassins*, and an Aretha CD, among others. He also was in charge of art for Superman and DC comics. I told him I wanted a logo and Neal asked what did I have in mind? My answer was easy. You know me. He came back with this:

All I said was, "It's me. It's Bryan. Perfect!"

LESSONS FROM MOM

STICKS AND STONES MAY BREAK MY BONES BUT WORDS WILL NEVER HURT ME.

I suppose this is one of the first lessons I learned. When kids would call me names, as all kids do (and I did, also), I would go home and tell mom and she would tell me this.

The first time I can say race came into it was from Lewis, a Jewish kid (this is important, here) I went to school with. On Saturdays, Glenn and I took a pottery class. I was seven or eight years old. We were the only kids of colour in a class of, say, maybe ten children.

One day, Lewis said I was brown or burnt because I stayed in the oven too long. Pottery class has ovens, remember. I told mom and out came the sticks and stones thing. I like to think that, had we been several years older, Lewis would not have used the oven bit. And had I been older, I certainly would have had a great retort to use.

LESSON ALERT. I'll say it as an adult. I don't give a royal blue fuck *whatcha* say about me.

16

HILLY'S.

When I learned about a cabaret club downtown in Greenwich Village, where you could come in and sing, I investigated. The club, Hilly's, was on 9th Street. It was named after Hilly Kristal, who went on to open the famous punk club, CBGB.

His wife – I refuse to give the cow any credit, so let's call her *'Karen'*, which is fitting for her – ran Hilly's and I went in and talked with her. The nobodies could come in on the slow nights and maybe do a song or two, while the folks who were in shows could perform whenever they wanted and do several songs. This is where I first came across Bette Midler, Daphne Davis, Dawn Hampton, and Baby Jane Dexter.

We also-rans would sit and wait, hoping to be blessed by *Karen*. Sometimes, we did not get on at all. But it was a learning process. I'd sit and watch the performers. I was 19 and I was happy in my new world.

One night, I was looking good, or so I thought: a nice sweater, shirt, scrubbed up. *Karen* came over and said she did not like what I had on, and she would not be putting me on. "Go home and try the next time." Mind you, it wasn't just me – she was a bitch to everyone. One of her own kids was suing her over Hilly's will when he died. In her obit, after *she* died, I forget who the famous punk singer was, but he and a few others had nothing nice to say about her.

That night, tail between my legs, I left. As I walked

towards the subway, I was crying. I went to a phone booth and called mom around 12 A.M. and told her what had just happened. The urge to go back and tell *Karen* a few choice words was building up inside of me.

Mom said, "**She doesn't need you. You need her**. Stop crying, come on home and go back the next time wearing a different sweater."

I did go back, and nothing was said about that night by either of us.

Shortly after, I got a part in an off-off-Broadway play called *Sweet Tom*. Picture in the paper. Write-ups etc. During the week, after the play, I would walk down 8th Street from the theater to Hilly's and sit there, waiting to go on and sing a number or two, depending upon *her* moods.

Then, someone told her I was in a show. I never told her. She comes over to me and it was as if I'd said the magic words and the gates to the castle had opened. "Bryan, why didn't you tell me you were in a show? How long have you been in it? Listen, any time you want to come in, I'll put you on right away, so you don't have to hang around. Do what you want. Come in on the weekends. It will be ok."

I was one of the chosen, now. I went home and told mom.

"See? Aren't you glad you didn't go back and curse her out, the way you wanted to? Isn't this much better – to have her suddenly need you so she can tell people, 'Oh, he's in a show'?"

YES, MOM.

LESSON ALERT. Patience. Which is not easy, being a Noo Yawker. We're the type of folks who yell at a micro-wave oven to hurry up!

When your hand is in the mouth of a lion, you ease it out. You don't jerk it out. Patience.

IT'S NOT MY JOB.

Mom believed that girls should know how to change a tire. Where the fuse box is. How to use a hammer and screwdriver. Fix little things. Boys should know how to cook. Sew on a button. Use a vacuum cleaner. She did not believe in gendered jobs.

I learned how to sew on a button at around five or so, and to use a sewing machine when I was ten. Not a home Singer – I'm talking a big factory machine. A power machine. I could sew curtains, shirts, pants, vests. You name it. I was a lazy sewer, mind you. I preferred straight seams, but yes, I could cut and sew a *Vogue* pattern. I would cry; but I could.

LESSON ALERT. Learn how to do many things. You never know.

NOT WHERE YOU EAT.

I cannot recall how this was brought up, but I do know it didn't have anything to do with me or something I had done (for a change).

Mom pointed out that our Labbie, Purlie, would go way up in the back of the yard when he had *to go,* but he'd play and eat close to the house.

This lesson came in very handy for me when I started working in clubs. I would never pick up anyone there. Not my style. This was my job. I was working. Yes, there were one or two guys over the years (I am being modest here, I like to think) who hit on me; but no, thank you.

Ok. Quick one. I was working in West Virginia. After the show, this cute young kid came over and tried. The club sold hot dogs. Could he buy me a hot dog? He was so cute about it. I'm thinking, aww, he's taking his school lunch money to buy me a hot dog. I thanked him, of course, but it was no, although I never even said the word "no".

I paid that lesson from mom forward to a couple of fellow performers. One was so excited, telling me about her new boyfriend and how she got him a job in the club, and they would be together all the time, etc. I told her, "Get him out. Get him a job in the supermarket, or picking up litter, or a job in another club. Get him out, for the sake of your relationship."

Well, a few months later, we ran into each-other and she

was sorry she didn't listen. They broke up. The usual BS. Lies, rumours, cheating, etc.

Another performer friend would drink and dabble in drugs with the owners. Again, I said, "This is your job. Go next door and do whatever, but not where you get paid. Debauch yourself into a stupor, but not where you work. This way, if anything goes bad, it's down to your work and not the recreational things."

He didn't get it. When clubs didn't hire him again, he took it badly. He didn't know why. I said, "If you kept it professional, then you'd know they didn't like your show – not because you drank too much or snorted more than your share, or you hit on the wrong guy."

LESSON ALERT: Don't shit where you eat.

IT CAN BE WORSE.

Mom had a positive attitude about life. No matter what was happening and how low things were, and could get, her bottom line was: I'm alive.

I keep that in my mind.

LESSON ALERT. It can always be worse. Be glad you're alive.

TOMORROW AIN'T PROMISED.

I believe this is the lesson I took away more than any of them. Tomorrow ain't promised. Do it today. Live today. Right now, with us all under house arrest of some sort, here is the lesson. All those things we were going to do tomorrow, next week, in a month or so – we can't.

Mother Gibbens, Roger's mother, gave us her beloved china dinner service. She said she wanted to see it being used now. Why wait for us to have it after she died?

Mom always said, "Give me my flowers now. Say those nice things now. Not after I'm gone."

I taught this lesson to Roger. It took him a while to understand it. When he became ill, he said he was glad he had embraced that ideal.

LESSON ALERT. Do it now. I live by that.

DON'T LET OTHERS TELL YOU HOW YOU SHOULD FEEL

Growing up, I was the fat kid. The one who couldn't run and play. Oh yeah, I was called fat. I told mom and she worked on that with me. Telling me I was a good boy and people don't have a right to call me names. When I got older and out into the world as a teenager, friends would attempt to fat-shame me and tell me how I should look. I needed to join a gym. Stop eating so much etc. Mom's words would pop into my head.

LESSON ALERT. My self-esteem does not fluctuate, depending upon the size of my belt.

IF IT SOUNDS TOO GOOD TO BE TRUE...!

On the way home from school one day, Glenn and I saw several kids crowding around a man. Nosey me wanted to know what was going on. The man was saying he was a talent scout for tv and movies and was looking for children to star in shows. Well!!!

He was taking names and phone numbers. He asked if our mother was home because he could come now and talk to her and tell her all about what he was looking for and we'd be perfect etc. I gave him our address and ran home to tell mom.

We ran in the door. "Mom! Mom!" We were jumping up and down, telling her about this talent scout "... And he's coming now to talk to you!"

The man comes and is talking to mom. I'm telling him I sing and dance. I do a little song for him. "We just did the show The King and I." Great. Great. Everything is good.

Just as he is about to go into the details of the costs, the bell rings and another man is standing there. He is part of the scam, asking to speak to mom, causing distraction. Says he is from school – the PTA – and needs to speak with her, blah, blah, blah. The talent agent comes to the door and jumps to mom's defence, raising his voice at the man, saying she is busy now – and to come back later. Trying to play her.

What the men did not know was that my mother was the secretary of the PTA!!!! Suck on that, guy.

He got back to the costs, and he just did the whole scam deal. Needless to say, he did not get a check from mom. When he left, Glenn and I were disappointed, of course, and mom sat us down and explained the scam to us.

That taught me, as a ten or eleven-year-old kid, to be a cautious consumer. A lesson never forgotten.

LESSON ALERT. If it sounds too good to be true, it is. And Roger taught me that when it comes to investing, too. BERNIE MADOFF sound familiar?

PUT ON EARTH TO TEACH AND HELP

One day, I don't know how it came up or what we were talking about, but mom said I was put on earth to teach and help. It might not be in a classroom, but that was my mission. At the time, I had no idea what she was on about. I was in my 20s, I think.

Mom kept a busy schedule, going here, doing that. Once

a year, she would take over a hall and invite about fifty of her friends for a breakfast/brunch affair. Usually, I was out of town and couldn't go. One time when I got back home, mom said the daughter of a friend was hoping to see me. She wanted to thank me for saving her when we were kids, ten years old.

"What?" I said.

"She was going to run away. She wasn't happy with her mother telling her what to do and having rules to follow."

"Huh?"

"You talked her out of running away by telling her all the bad things that could happen to her. How her family would miss her."

"I did that?" Mind you, I still do not recall doing that; nor do I recall the girl.

"Yes, so she said. And she was always grateful to you."

"Good… I guess. Glad I could help."

Ok. So, I was helping at ten years old. Now let us skip ahead.

I was working in Key West. I knew the manager of the bar, but I hadn't seen in him since 1971. This was 15 years later, and he reminded me that I saved him from OD-ing. I had forgotten.

Another day, I was reading a newspaper and there was an article about a man who had M.S. and HIV but was not letting it get to him. Looking at the photo, I realized I knew him. Marty. We were friends of friends and had lost touch. A nice guy. I called the paper and said I wanted to get in touch with Marty and would they forward my number to him? A few days later, he called. After a brief chat, we arranged to meet. Marty said I'd saved his life. We had been at the Continental Baths and I saved him from drowning in the pool. He had taken drugs and slipped under the water. I got him out of the pool, dressed him, took him home and stayed with him till he came out of it.

In England, after my show, a man who has since become a friend was a bad drinker. He questioned me as to why I don't drink. How do I have fun? **Do** I have fun? Did I ever drink? NO. It never appealed to me. I had no interest in drinking. In school, the kids would drink and smoke and one might tell me that I didn't want to be cool. Ya got that right. No, I didn't. To shorten this long story, my friend has been sober for 30 years. He told my cousin he owed his changing his life around to me. I had merely answered his questions truthfully.

I helped another friend kick coke, by showing him all the bad things ahead of him. He did.

I've always believed that when the pupil is ready, the teacher will appear.

When I started working, there was an amazing performer doing drag. He was fantastic. Beautiful costumes, excellent on stage. He was very popular, with a loyal following. The problem he had was his drinking and drugtaking, and all the hangers-on around him. One day, we were alone in the dressing room, and I asked him why he had to be like this. What was the good? He was getting fired from places. People would not hire him due to his off-stage antics which were now *on* stage with him. He had no answer. I said, "You must stop this crap. You're too good." He agreed and promised he was going to change.

Sadly, he didn't. We ran into each other one day, crossing Broadway in New York. He looked like hell. A shame to see him looking like that. He said he just couldn't stop all the bad stuff and was nearly homeless and down-and-out and he remembered our talk and said he was sorry about it. I wished him luck and hoped things would change for him. I heard he died not too long after that, and people raised money to bury him. So sad.

Sometimes when the teacher appears, the student is playing hooky that day.

There are other instances in my life where I've helped or tried to help others. Ok, mom. I suppose you were right.

LESSON ALERT. Teach and help. My lot in life.

Here is an example of my mother. After I fell and my arthritis flared, I was in the hospital. One night, a kid about my age, 9 or so, was admitted. His name was Arnold. He had been hit by a car. Luckily, not badly.

The next day, mom came to visit and she met Arnold. His father came in later. Arnold was in a hospital gown. Same thing the next day. Hospital gown. Mom went and bought a pair of pjs in a size my thigh couldn't even fit in.

When Arnold's father came, still no pjs for Arnold. Mom explained she'd purchased the wrong size for me – YEAH, RIGHT – and she made some excuse about not being able to return them, but if it was ok with the father, Arnold could have them. He thanked mom. Arnold now had a pair of jammies.

Mom wanted, and tried, to save the world. I have many more instances of her largesse.

I had grief counseling after Roger died, and the therapist said, "Tell me about your mother". I went from tears to a huge smile. She commented how I lit up.

I was working out on Fire Island for a weekend gig. I took mom out with me. I made her several caftans of various styles and materials and told her what jewelry to wear with each. (Lord, I'm so gay).

One night, I looked out my room door – and there was mom, sitting in a beach chair by the pool, holding court with several guys sitting on the deck, talking with her. The next day, a woman said she had breakfast with my mother and told her how lovely it was to see her there, supporting me. Mom said, "Of course! He's my son."

Several people told me how lucky I was to have a mother like that. I offered to give her to them. Very lucky.

The most important lesson I learned from mom is unconditional love. I was her son. End of. No matter whatever happened in my life, I was her son and she loved me, no matter. She may not like or approve of some of the things I might do, but the love would always be there. Always. On Mother's Day, I would send her a congratulations card for being my mother!

FRIENDS. AND NOT THE TV SHOW

A friend is the one who comes to bail you out of jail after a night out. A *really* good friend is the one sitting next to you in the cell, who says, "Damn, that was fun."

I used to go to the beach after a night working. I'd go home, sleep a bit, then hit the sand around 6 A.M. and watch the Concorde fly over as it landed at J.F.K. One time, as I was half dozing, a guy comes over to me and asks if I'm Bryan Murphy, the performer. Yes. Guilty. He had seen my show several times.

His name was Glenn. We started meeting at the beach occasionally. He came straight from his job at the Brooklyn Battery Tunnel. A friendship developed. Glenn and I would hang out. He was as insane as me. I convinced him to go skydiving several times. He bought his motorcycle and we would hit the road. Whitewater rafting. Fun things.

One summer, he'd auditioned for a singing group. Glenn got the part of the Leather Man in Village People.

This was inspirational for me, as he travelled the world. He'd send me postcards. Or we'd catch up when he was back home and he'd tell me about some of the places he had been. I began to search out places to work. Over the years, we'd meet all over America. Then came Europe and Australia. I knew one of the other guys in Village People before he joined and Glenn introduced me to Alex, the army man. I had so much fun.

Glenn and I could talk on the phone for hours. His mother would go to bed and when she woke up the next morning, we were still talking about everything. I learned to look at both sides of a discussion. What amazed both of us – we could see the same thing and have totally different ideas. Social, history, music, show biz, life, gay stuff – it didn't matter, he and I could go at it. I miss him greatly, and our conversations, which could go on till bedtime and resume when we woke up. My friend Phil and I can get into deep chats, as I did with Glenn – however, he is in LA. Sadly, we don't get a chance often.

I owe it to Glenn for introducing me to Tina Turner. She played the Ritz in New York, at the start of her solo career. Glenn and Alex got me, Kathy and my horn player into her dressing room after her performance. I gave her my Bryan Fan Club pin. She graciously put it on.

One day, I was in a bookstore looking at books on Tina, and there were the photos of that night and my pin on her top.

This wasn't my first time talking to her, though. I went to a private showing of *Thank God It's Friday* and Tina was there. I chatted briefly with her after the movie. The party for the film was being held at Studio 54. As I got to the door, the gate-keeper opened the rope and said, "Hello Bryan. Good to see you. Enjoy the evening."

Knocked me with a feather! I was expecting to tell him who I was and explain I was on the list, etc. So maybe I was sorta well known. And this was before I even performed there. Later that evening, I danced with Tina.

MY BEST FRIEND GAYLE, AS OPRAH SAYS,

Talking about her friend, Gayle King. Well, I have a *best friend Gayle,* too. Kathy. She is my bestie, my bffffffffffffffffff forever, as I love to remind her. There is no one walking the earth or circling the moon who knows me better. We first met when she was singing in a group at a show room where I was doing the tech. Later on, she was a server at another room, Scene One, where I performed. We hit it off. That began the deep connection between us.

For roughly eight years, she travelled with me as I worked. Ernie, the boyfriend, called her my road manager. And to some extent, she was. Kathy would go with the DJs and run my show. We were on the road all the time. Hotels, planes, buses, cars. Up and down and across the eastern half of the US. Non-stop, it seemed. One year, I think we were home maybe 4 months, in total.

Kathy got to see things some people should never see in a few of the places I worked. All I recall is we were laughing and laughing all the time. We continued our travelling until she decided it would be nice to sleep in the same bed every night and maybe have a normal life. She went on to become an executive in the marketing field.

Due to the time difference, we speak several times a week by phone/zoom.

Being intuitive, Kathy is the one who pointed out that I got sick much more often living in the UK than I ever did at home in New York. I hadn't thought of it before she mentioned it. I was getting colds all the time. I did some research on it and sure enough, my body was not used to the various germs in England and it would take time to build up my immunity to them.

My bff Kathy is always there for me and I'm grateful she is in my life. When she reads this, she will throw the book across the room.

Kathy also made me aware how similar my life was to Tina Turner, in a way.

Tina began chanting when her life was hell.

I started to meditate, thanks to my friend Thom, when I was dealing with the death of many people around me. And I add that my daily meditation has certainly helped to preserve my equanimity since March 2020 – that's for sure. Thank you, Thom.

Tina moved to Europe. I did.

Tina was surprised that when she first performed in Europe, the audience sang with her.

Me too, when they sang with me. In the UK, I think it harkens back to the age of music hall. I was used to people sitting and listening to me. If I wanted them to sing along with me, I'd tell them.

Tina got a European boyfriend, then husband. I did.

She had property on both continents, as did I.

When she left Ike, she was in debt from all the show cancellations. I had a failed concert due to backer problems, and had to work to pay everything back, myself.

Tina retired and said she wanted solitude. This lockdown has forced it upon me. And I'm loving it. LOVING IT.

Due to her health, she cannot sign autographs any longer. For me, it's not autographs, but due to my health, I can't hold a pen. Using a folk is difficult, but THAT I CAN DO. No surprise there.

Luckily, I think that is all I want to have in common with her. She has had some horrible trouble, the last couple of years. One being her several serious health problems, suicide of her son, death of her mother and sister. I will happily settle just for my gout and advancing arthritis, thank you very much.

Now, wouldn't it be nice if the next thing like Tina I have is my book turned into a movie and a musical. I can live with that.

BELLOWS FALLS - OR FELLOW'S... as they sometimes said.

I met Thom Herman when I worked for him at his Andrew's Inn, in Bellows Falls, Vermont. The inn had one of the best rooms to work. I loved performing there. The weekends were hectic but come Monday and Tuesday, things would go quiet and Thom and I would chat and exchange ideas on things. He became a major part of my life.

When I was experiencing trouble with sick and dying friends and trying to come to terms and calm myself, Thom introduced me to meditation. I will say, it has been wonderful for me. I've been meditating since the early 90s.

Thom was a great help, checking up on me during Roger's illness and after. He married me and Roger on the dock in front of a ship in Boston. Thank you for taking care of me – mind, body and soul, Thom.

BUGS BUNNY

I have no idea why, but Bugs Bunny spoke to me. His self-esteem. His confidence. He has been my hero since I was a kid. I'd watch his show every Saturday morning and I do believe, subtly, I got his message. I was able to read between the lines. Never give up. Never take anyone's guff. Stand up for yourself.

In all of Bugs' cartoons, he never came out the loser and

in the ONLY ONE where he might not have been the total winner, he turned that into a plus. Ahh, yes. Bugs is my hero.

The Bugs Bunny quotes that I use:
1. You know of course, this means war.
2. He don't know me *bery* well, do he?
3. And furthermore, stop breathing in my cup.
4. If I do dat, I get a whippin'. I do dat!
5. Think fast, Rabbit.
6. Low Bridge. – This is the one I use all the time. It means, 'Move, excuse me, watch out'. I like to see the reaction I get when I say it on crowded elevators.

NATURE V. NURTURE

CONFIDENCE

This is a discussion where no one seems able to say what the definitive answer is. There is going to be a number of examples of *Nature* vs. *Nurture* from my life, in this book.

Glenn, my brother, and I were born 18 months apart. I am the oldest. When I was at the age to learn something, he got a heads-up on the lesson.

I recall reading that when choosing a puppy out of a litter, you should try to pick the one who comes to you, or is trying to get out of the cage or climb over the fence. According to my mother, I broke my crib. Probably trying to escape. Or eat it. Ha.

You see some children holding on to daddy's leg or hiding behind mother's skirt. I was not that kid. Not me. For me, it was, "Move. You're blocking my view. I can't see." I was always getting into things. I would ask questions. I was curious. Still am. I could not wait for my mother to go if she were leaving. However, Glenn would start crying if she were not in his direct sight-line. Not peripheral, but direct. I was the little angel when she was around. But...!

I had confidence from an early age. Glenn, sadly, not so much. To my mind, it was always there. Yes, I can say my confidence was instilled in me by my mom. Well, mom and my mentor, Bugs Bunny. Throw in as sub-mentors Charlie Chan, Sherlock Homes, Miss. Marple, Mr. Moto. Detective shows where you had to use your brains to solve the crimes.

I've always been a confident person. Confident, not cocky. Huge difference.

I'm not sure at what age we were travelling on buses by ourselves, but I'm willing to say I was six years old. Mom would put us on the bus to go to church for Sunday School and she would come down later for the eleven o'clock service. Straight route. Maybe 10-15 minutes. A few times, ladies would ask us, "Little boys, do you know where you're going?"

My answer was, "I don't know the street, but I'll know it when I see it." And I did.

I was travelling on the subway alone when I was nine years old. Loved it. This gives a kid great confidence. A parent knows when the child is ready for things. Or should. I was ready, willing, and able and couldn't wait to get out there and explore the world. One year I got a bike for Christmas, I was gone. Freedom.

From time to time, after I finished working at a club out of town, someone would tell me to be careful going to the car or to my hotel. I'd tell them, "Hey, I'm from New York. I'm good."

I do believe the song *New York, New York* is so right – 'If you can make it there, you can make it anywhere'. That applies to so much in life. Confidence. And throw in the Brooklyn part – wow.

Let's talk confidence. This confidence thing spread over into my working life, thank goodness.

I've never done well with a *no* answer. A performer friend was shocked how I would call clubs and challenge them to hire me. He listened to me on the phone with one. I said, "Hi, I'm calling for my semi-monthly answer of 'No you're not going to book me'." It was a call; didn't bother me.

Another club owner would say no all the time. Finally, he did say yes. The show was great. I asked him afterwards why he decided to book me. He responded: he got tired of saying no to me. We had a wonderfully long-term working relationship.

In my acting, I would walk into an audition or casting, do what I needed to do, then walk out and not think about it. They call me, they call me. I had a friend who would go to an audition, then go home and he would sit by the phone. This was before cell phones. Not allow anyone to use it, in case the casting folks should call. And you wonder why a number of performers end up on drugs, drinking and self-destruction? Being a performer is a vicious life. He could not understand my way of thinking. Sure, I wanted the job, but I was not about to let it control me.

One time, I had a cold and had taken to my bedchamber. Phone rang and it was Ed, my agent. Casting people want to see me for a tv show this afternoon.

I dragged myself out of my sick bed; went in. I was playing an FBI agent. I did what they asked. Left, went home, and thought nothing of it, since I'd done the best I could and went back to my bed. Phone rings; I say, "Take a message, I'm not moving".

Roger says I got the job. Great. That job was with one of the Spice Girls.

Ok. Only one time did I not get a job and was evil about it. Ed called and said the casting people wanted to see me the next day. He gave me the breakdown as to what they wanted. I went in and did very well. Had them laughing and they were pleased. I was almost assured. They called Ed and said they were 99% sure it was me. Don't you know? They turned me down for a famous American tv person! I was annoyed and pissed off about that one. Perhaps I should be flattered I was dumped only because he was famous. GGGGGRRRRRRRRRRR. Oh, well. Show biz.

I did a commercial with THE HOFF. That guy from that beach show – David Hasseloff. They gave me a man bun. Coveralls. Face made up. Middle of summer. Hot as hell. Waiting all day. Shoot time, I said my lines – and all they shot was my hand!!! My ring was a star. Ahh, show biz.

I was asked if I would shave my hair for a commercial.

NOPE! Casting agents wanted me because I was an American. I get there, and suddenly, will I do a British accent? Duh, you asked me to come in because you were looking for a Yank. Make up your minds! Such fun.

Confidence. AS LONG AS I AM PREPARED, I rarely doubt *me*. I may doubt a situation, but not my ability to deal with it, usually. That was to come when Roger got sick.

This is what is in the back of my use of the word 'fuck' or any derivation of it. Go – yourself. – off. – you, etc. If one uses it, that means you must be prepared to deal with the consequences. It says, "I'm ok and can take whatever comes my way." My theory is, as long as it *ain't* the big red button in Washington, it doesn't matter. And IF it IS the big red button in Washington, it WON'T matter.

I like a confident woman, too. Broads. Not dainty precious ladies that would faint at the sight of a mouse or run screaming and jump on a chair if they saw an insect. Now mind you, some of the creepy crawlies they have in Australia, I'd be on the chair with her. A woman who would take a bottle of beer and hit it on the tabletop to open it. Not the lady who drank sherry out of a cutesy little glass while holding her pinky up. I want Molly Brown, taking command of the rowboat as the Titanic sank.

I was never into the vulnerability of Marilyn Monroe or Judy Garland. I do appreciate their talent. I was more Joan Crawford with a gun-belt slung low across her hips in *Johnny Guitar* than Joanie walking into the sea in the film,

Humoresque. In an evening gown, yet. I like the lady who has a gun strapped to her thigh underneath that evening gown.

Since this preference started before I was of school age and able to reason, I think it was normal and natural for me.

I hated watching movies where the girl runs from the bad guy and always trips. This annoyed me to no end. Give me Annie Oakley, Sheena, Queen of the Jungle. I did not care about Roy Rogers – I wanted Dale Evens to shoot the bank robbers. While my brother watched war movies, women's roller derby on telly on a Saturday afternoon excited me. Thank heaven they did not have women in bikinis wrestling in jello when I was a teenager in those days. Who knows how I might have turned out?

As I said to Dame Diana Rigg about her role on the show, *The Avengers*, "On behalf of every 13, 14-year-old boy, thank you for Ms. Peel."

SUMMERTIME AND THE LIVING *AIN'T* EASY

For me, the summer meant swimming every day. I loved to swim. I think, in another life, I was a fish. Probably a shark. If – and that's a big if – I had thought of it, and wasn't lazy and undisciplined, I might have tried to get into the Olympics, for swimming.

As with all kids, or most, anyway, summer is the next best time of year after Christmas. No school. Yea! Some kids go to day camp; other kids to go grandma & family; while lots of children go away to camp. And from my point of view, the lucky ones stay home. That is what I liked to do. However, dear Ms. Murphy, my mother, had another idea. Still to this day, terrifies me to talk about it.

One year – I think I was coming out of fourth grade – she announced that Glenn and I were going away to the country for the summer. Country? What does that mean? I quit the scouts when they mentioned overnight camping, outdoors. Bears outdoors. Toilets outdoors, Showers outdoors. Sleeping in tents outdoors. What is country? The visions were scary. Little did I know.

Mom had a friend of a friend – now, right there, she had lost me – who lived in the country. The country being some one-horse town in New Jersey. And 'town' was being kind.

Ok, I'll start from the beginning if I can get through it.

School ended and a few days later, we headed for this place. One subway, one long bus ride out of New York City, away from my home.

This is a movie set. Cue the dueling banjos music.

We arrive at this wooden shack, which is the stop for the bus. There is a metal Coke ice box. Screen door to the shack. It is July and hot. Mom has us dressed up, as usual. We go inside. There are no lights on. One fan in the ceiling, spreading hot air.

Can you hear the banjos yet?

Mom tells the man behind the counter that we want to go

to this location. He has one of the men who is sitting there in the plastic porch chair drive us, in his broken-down car, to the house in the country.

Oh, did I mention there are no streets, no sidewalks, no cement curbs? Dirt roads. Fields. Scarecrows.

We headed towards this place. As he was driving, I'm making a mental note of landmarks. A tree, here. A cow, there. Oh, over there is a barn. Memorising what is where and how to get back to the place where the bus stops, in case I have to make a break for it and run. My brother was on his own.

We arrive and are met by Miss Berta.

My nightmare had begun. The house was large. Three floors. Everything was dusty because the roads were dirt roads. Hang onto your hats. No tv. No phone. And here it comes – the toilet was outside. OUTSIDE! A hole in the ground inside a wooden shack. Bathroom? Nope. A round tin tub in the middle of the kitchen on Saturday night, after you boil the water. Oh, have I mentioned there was no running water? It came from outside, from something called a pump. And you had to *prime* it. Whatever that meant. What hell was my mom leaving me in?

There were kids running all over the place. Miss Berta had a million grandchildren. No shoes, dirty old t shirt and short pants were *de rigueur*. I, who had a white dinner jacket, black patent leather shoes and kid-skin gloves at the age of six. I was dying, here.

Mom said goodbye, promising she would be back, and for us to have fun and enjoy it. Was she kidding?

Enjoy servitude, at such a tender young age? All the kiddies had chores. Dishes, cleaning the floors that were dusty the moment you finished. I had to feed those feathered things. Get their eggs. Pick vegetables and fruit. I hated it. Sweat, dusty and hot. Hated it.

Only two good things, to me – one was the food, and I learned how to ride a big bike. I think I was still trying to formulate how to get out of Dodge anyway I could.

Cue the music for Jaws.

One day, we were going to go to the supermarket in the city. New York? No. Trenton. I figured there must be a way to get home from there. Just in case.

I had a habit of wolf-whistling at pretty ladies, back home. Usually the response was, "Oh, how cute!" Or they'd call me "Fresh!" Always a positive reaction.

We're walking along the street – me, Miss Berta, a couple of her sons and a dozen or so of her grandbrats. I whistled at this pretty lady and it was freeze-frame. Everything stopped, suddenly. They snatched me by the hand, my feet did not touch the ground, and they threw me into the car and all of us high-tailed it out of town, in several cars.

No one ever said a word to me as to what, why, when, where, or how come. I never knew what had gone on. I simply forgot about it. It was back to a horrible, unhappy, hot summer for me.

I have no idea how long we were imprisoned with Miss Berta. One day, she told us mom was coming and we were going home. I don't think I slept till she arrived. I was so happy, I was willing to put on my suit, tie, etc. just to leave.

We got home and mom had redecorated. Our room was nice and had some sort of wall design on it. There were a couple of new games for us. It was great to be where I belonged. Now, my friends can understand me when I say I only like concrete, steel and glass. That summer with grass, fields, corn stalks and animal smells traumatized me.

As we neared the end of school the following year, I announced that if she sent me back to Miss Berta, I was running away. And that was that. Believe me, my weak threat is not the reason we did not go – I was having trouble with what turned out to be arthritis and mom decided it was best I stay home. I ended up in the hospital for two weeks.

Many years later, I asked mom why she sent us there. She said she thought it was best for us to be away from the city and see another way of life in the country. Fresh air – and all that was B.S., as far as I was concerned.

Fast-forward to my teen years, and I was learning about the murder of the 14-year-old Black boy, Emmett Till, in 1955. He was kidnapped, tortured, lynched, and dumped in the Tallahatchie River for whistling at a white lady. I also read about the KKK activity in Southern New Jersey. Now, it all made sense to me. I understood why our shopping trip to Trenton was abruptly cancelled and they grabbed me, and we got out of town. So sad. So sad.

Speaking of sad, I hadn't thought of this until I started writing the book.

I don't recall his name, but there was a boy who would meet us and he, Glenn and I would walk to school together. This one day, for some reason, mom had somewhere to go and left before us. She made breakfast and told us to clean off the table when we were through.

The boy climbed up the steps and knocked on the window to let us know he was there. We jumped up and were about to scrape the plate into the garbage because Mom had made the toast a little burned, so we were not going to eat it. Of course, now, I love food that is on the burned side, but not then. The boy asked if we were going to eat the toast. "No." So, could he have it? "Yes, sure." He was hungry and we were about to throw food away. That saddens me. I don't know what happened to him, but he did not stay the entire year.

BORN UNDER A RAINBOW

We've all heard of stories of people that we say were born under a cloud. No matter what happens in the world, it's always worse for them. If it's bad, you know it's going to happen to them. Just like the character, Pigpen, in the comic strip, Peanuts. He walks around with a cloud over him.

I was, or always felt I was, born under a rainbow. In fact, a double rainbow. I had a fantastic childhood. As mom said, we got everything we needed and *some* of what we wanted. And I wanted a lot! But I'm sure that comes as no surprise to anyone who knows me.

Here are three amazing examples of being born under a rainbow.

When Glenn and I were young, before school age, grandma sent us to the candy store on the corner, probably to buy the newspaper. There were no streets to cross. Two to three minutes away from her home. On the way back, we passed several stores, one being a large paint store. We got to the next store front and there was a huge crash and loud noises behind us. A garbage truck went right into the storefront. What? Five seconds after we passed it?

One day, coming from the bakery, a man flew past me, running – as if running for his life. He had his hat in his hand and I was a couple of feet from him. I thought nothing of it until I looked up toward the other end of the block – and standing there, was a man with a pistol in his hand. He had been firing at the man that ran by me. I must have been nine or ten.

Fast forward many, many years later. I was on my way home. Nice quiet Sunday afternoon. I crossed the street, got to the other side and heard a big bang. I turned around and a car had come up on the sidewalk and rammed into the fence I had just passed.

Lesson here: don't go to the store. Stay indoors.

If I were a cat, that would mean I have six lives left, so I'm still ahead of the game if that is the case.

Now of course, if you want to add the fact that I used to stick hair pins in the electric socket, that would mean I have five left! Ahh, kids.

GEORGE ORWELL HAD 1984.
PRINCE, 1999.
AMERICA HAD 1777.
I HAD 1964.

had three major life-changing events happen to me in 1964. First, I lost my ally against my mom. My grandma died. The first death close to me. I say 'ally' because grandparents are the ones who spoil you and always take your side against the *enemy*. She had always been in my life. She was a great cook and loved to feed me. Glenn and I would stay with grandma often, especially during the summer holiday.

I credit my grandma for my imagination. She was not a tv fan and did not have one. And of course, as kids, we lived for television. Grandma would listen to the radio. In the evenings, after dinner, we'd sit in the dark and listen to the radio. Some of them went on to become tv shows. During the day – again, no tv – I'd lie across the bed and look out the window at people going about their lives. Glenn and I would invent stories about the people we saw. Looking back, it was a fun time. I do think that was what helped me to work on building characters later in my working life.

The second event was going to high school. I was in the

last half of the second term when, suddenly, things changed with the New York City school system. Instead of three years in middle school, now, it would be two. This was supposed to help desegregate schools. Yeah, right!

We were given five choices of high schools to pick from. I chose the new high school, Canarsie. I would be part of the first students in the school. I had no interest in any of the other schools. In order of preference, I wrote 'Canarsie' down on lines one to five. You don't ask, you don't get. One or two schools were closer, but I wanted Canarsie. I got Canarsie. I never discovered if it helped that my mother was on the local school board, or not. But I got what I wanted.

Come September, I went out a few days early, to see how to get there and check out my new school. The parents in the area were not happy that "kids from out of the area" (read: "Black kids") were being bussed in. I did not care. I'd got Canarsie.

The first day of school, I got on the bus and the train and another bus to my new high school. Well, the parents were out in full force. Picket signs and all. As I entered the grounds, one of mothers holding up her sign said to me, "We're doing this because of you!" Years later, when my school class was talking about getting together for a reunion, and what it was like for us the first day in a new school, I brought up *my* first day at Canarsie – and one of the students apologized to me for it. That was kind of her.

The last life-altering thing to come into my life in 1964

was the SUPREMES. The Supremes. My life revolved around Mary, Diana, and Flo. I ate, slept, walked, breathed, talked about The Supremes. Nothing else mattered to me but the Supremes.

The Beatles were out that year also, and some of my friends went that route. Not me. My bestie from school, Henry, and I were controlled by The Supremes. We read, watched, collected, listened to everything we could find about The Supremes. Sadly, I missed out on a few of their early appearances in New York because I was too young to go. Or rather, mom would not allow me to go. As soon as I was old enough, I went to every concert. I bought every poster and program they had. Artist merchandise marketing was still a few years away, or who knows how many boxes of things I would have had? I collected Supreme memorabilia for years. When I left New York, I had about twenty boxes of Supremes stuff. I gave it to another Supremes fan.

I would fantasize about meeting them. Working with them. Hanging out with them. I would talk about them to anyone who was within earshot. Going back to our school reunion, a classmate asked me if I still was in love with The Supremes. This was 40-something years later. That led me to believe that I HAD BEEN OBSESSED, for her to recall it all those years later.

Little did I know that The Supremes were to play a huge part in my career-planning further down the road.

For the graduating class, my school held a career day.

People from various professions were invited to visit and talk to the students who signed up for their talk. Some of the talks would be finance, sports, education, computers, police, fireman, and on and on. We were given a list and could choose two or three for the day. I chose entertainment.

My music teacher was friends with Mercer Ellington, Duke's son, who was a musician. He came and talked to us. The other class I chose was headed by a famous Brooklyn comedian, Morty Gunty. He told us about getting the trades (showbiz newspapers) every week and reading them. This way, we'd learn how things worked. What to do, what not to do. From my point of view, I was on my way. I now had a portal into the world of show business.

I knew I would need photos. And who did I pick to take my first professional 8x10 photos? James J. Kriegsmann, the celebrity and theatrical photographer – one of the best in the country. But none of that meant anything to me. It was because he was the photographer of the Supremes. **THE SUPREMES!** This was not the first step for me having some connection to my girls. In one of my shots, I even used a prop that they had used.

I was a star, in my mind. Using a photographer such as James J.

In New York City, there was an all-city high school chorus, made up of singers from all of the city high schools. Every year, they would perform at Lincoln Center. My music teacher in school suggested I audition for it. I went, for once feeling very cocky. I just knew I'd get in. Well! Everyone had to sing the same two lines from the song, *Just A Song At Twilight*. My turn, I sang my two lines.

The teacher in charge said, "Oh, you're a crooner."

I had no idea what that was. I smiled.

He said, "Thank you, but NO!"

What? He said no?!

Tail between my legs, I went home and told mom. I told her what I had to sing. She said she knew the song.

Monday, my music teacher asked how it went. I told her what happened. She wrote a note to the teacher in charge of that chorus and said for me to go back the following Saturday. Mom sang the song with me the whole week. Saturday, I went back – not as a crooner, but as a choral singer. I got it.

As I walked the halls to the stage at Lincoln Center, this was my first link to the Supremes. They had walked this hallway and performed on the same stage the year before. That show was produced by Trude Heller, who I would work for ten years later.

Still to come, was meeting them in New York at their hotel. Walking over to Mr. Gordy, President of Motown Records, and telling him I was a singer and hoped to someday sing with Miss Ross. He was kind and did not have his security kick me out of the room. Being in Miss Ross' suite in her opening week as a solo, at the Empire Room in the Waldorf. Lunch with the Supremes in London, thanks to Rick Gianatos, the music producer. And chatting on the phone with Mary from time to time. Giving Cindy a quarter so she could buy candy in the Americana Hotel. My girls. *"The girls"* as Ed Sullivan mistakenly called them, when he couldn't remember *The Supremes* as he introduced them.

I'm still having a tough time with losing Mary Wilson this year. The last time I saw her, she was doing a play in New York. It was me, my friend Glenn, and a friend of his. Mary and I were talking about the lady who introduced us, centuries before. Mary is gone. Difficult.

Interestingly, I was music, my brother was sports. I was in the all-city chorus. My brother was in the all-city football team. This is how he got the scholarship to Ohio State University. A famous reporter wrote a half-page newspaper article on Glenn and his football prowess. I have a trophy he was awarded for his outstanding playing ability.

MUSIC AND ME

Growing up, there was always music in the house. Mom had the radio on. She would sing. We had a piano that I would bang on.

I recall the first time that I heard people singing from the radio. The radio was a big white box with a gold grille and large round dial, sitting on top of the buffet. I was just tall enough to see under the radio. I can still see myself looking under the radio, trying to look in back of it. I could not figure where the people who were singing were. It amazed me.

Mom had a friend, Mrs. Cox. She was a music teacher, church choir leader, and religious. Whenever she came for dinner, she would say grace for what seemed like hours. She was blessing everyone at the table, mom for cooking it, me and Glenn for setting the table. The man at the supermarket who stocked the shelves. She blessed the farmer who raised the cow, and his wife for tilling the fields for the veggies. And heaven forbid she should forget John Deere, the man who invented the tractor, which aided the farm hands in ploughing the lower 40! I probably would have lost consciousness if I hadn't been so hungry. By the time she was through, the gravy had congealed and the flies waiting around for the scraps we would put in the garbage had dive-bombed to their deaths, from starvation.

However, when it came to music, Mrs. Cox was top drawer. She is the one responsible for me loving classical music. I thank her for that, but I'm not too sure if I forgive her for making me wait to eat.

I must have been six or seven when she took me to a classical concert. We were a few rows back from the front. The lady who would be singing appeared on stage. She was the ideal, in my mind, of a classical singer. Beautifully dressed, hair styled. Tall, her hands clasped in front of her. She struck a diva pose.

Then, the lady began to sing. Mrs. Cox was to my right. I tapped her on the shoulder, and whispered, "I can't understand her!"

I will always remember how she responded: "You listen to the beautiful sounds."

And that, folks, was the beginning of my love for classical music. That, and the music from Bugs Bunny cartoons. He used classical music in many of his shows.

As time went on, Mrs. Cox took over my music training by exposing me to other musical genres. Every year, there was a gospel choir weekend that she would attend. Choirs from all over the USA would come together and sing. Think of it like the movie *Pitch Perfect*, but with God's music. This one year, it was being held in Connecticut. I think I was maybe 12 or 13, and we went up for the weekend.

Every night and most of Saturday, these choirs would get a time-slot for them to perform. The hall was jumping. I loved it. I was (if you will excuse me saying it this way)... I was in heaven. Although I could happily do without the preachy stuff that went on at the beginning and in between acts. I got to see and hear and meet some famous gospel singers. The choir robes were flying, the piano and organ were hopping. It was great.

In school, we were offered various musical instrument classes. My brother chose the viola. I went for the piano. I don't recall where Glenn got lessons, or how. Since we had the piano at home, Mrs. Cox found me a piano teacher – Mrs. Noble was her name. Poor dear. She was so old, she probably baby-sat Chopin and Mozart. She must have weighed 80 pounds. She was so thin her veins were on the outside of her skin. But she could make a piano tinkle, I'll tell you.

Each week, she'd come to the house and ask me if I'd practiced. I, of course, said yes. The minute I sat down and began, she knew I hadn't opened the book since she'd left, the week before. This went on every week. Mrs. Noble would come. I faked it. When time was up, I'd give her the check mom left for her. Finally, she thought mom could do better things with her money than support the piano teacher of a student who did not want lessons. End of that piano teacher. And the end of Mrs. Cox and my music education. She had put me on a path, and it was now up to me.

MADAM MAUDE B. TAYLOR

I still wasn't done with the piano; however, it would soon be done with me. I wanted to play, but didn't want to practice – but ain't that always the case? Mom had a friend whose daughter was taking piano with a Madam Taylor. So, off I went to Madam Taylor.

She was this very starched, upright, covered-in-black-lace woman. Madam Taylor had a music school: several rooms in a brownstone building in Brooklyn. Music coming out from everywhere. Upstairs from where I was banging on the piano, there was singing. I was interested in that, too. The singing classes were run by her daughter, Ms. Gloria DeNard (who died, age 93, in 2020). She went on to be a jazz singer, recording artist, and started her own music school in Harlem.

Madam Taylor was strict. The one major thing I can recall from lessons with her was how my hands should be placed when playing. I was putting them straight out with a little curve to the fingers, and she wanted rounded hands. Our first conflict. I'm sure if she ever saw how Aretha placed her hands on the piano, Madam Taylor would freak.

Once I'd learned the melody of what I was playing, I was done with the music sheet. This was the beginning of the end, for me and the piano. I was playing by ear. I liked the music. She wanted me to read and play what was in front of me – to follow what was on the page and not what was in my mind. I wanted to play it how I felt it at the time – hold a note longer if I wanted, or play faster, or just play by vibrations. The end.

I don't recall how long she and I were at odds with my hands and reading music. Perhaps a couple of months, but we broke up. It was her idea. Looking back on it, she was not the type of teacher I needed. Nor I the type of pupil she wanted!

Years later, it hit me – the type of teacher that would work for me. Someone who would have realized what I was doing. Playing instinctively. That type of teacher would say, "Bryan, I see how you want to play, but how about you learning what is on the page? Then, once you have that, play it the way you want. But learn it properly, first."

Now, if Madam Taylor had said that to me, I might have gone on, stuck with the piano, and who knows where that might have led me? Playing piano in some dive, late at night, for all the drinks and cigarettes I could bum from folk. Then, at closing time, I'd head back to my one-room studio over an all-night deli. Ahh, the drama. The life I *coulda* had, if it hadn't been for Madam Taylor and my damn hands.

Whenever I hear *Fur Elise* by Beethoven, I think of Madam Taylor. It seemed there was always a student playing it. We must have had the same appointment time.

MS. DeNARD

After Madam Taylor suggested I do something else, some*where* else, I went up the stairs to Ms. DeNard's singing class and lessons. I think I was 10 or 11 by now. Ms. DeNard was fun. She wouldn't let you get away with anything, though. But boy, did she fall very far from Madam Taylor's tree. And that is proven by the fact that she went on to become a famous jazz singer.

I was taught the proper way to breathe when singing. That's something I've been troubled by my entire career, because I'm lazy.

Once a year, Madam Taylor's music school would put on a concert with the students from the various classes at the Brooklyn Academy of Music. Here again, as I look back, I was listening to music and not words. The song I chose to sing was *Stout Hearted Men...* (STOP IT!) I loved the intro to it. The big chords. The big sound.

The night of the performance, I stepped forward for my solo. The pianist started playing the song. I got lost in the music in this gigantic theater. I'd never heard the song sound so good. Ms. DeNard was standing in front of the stage, to conduct. Well, Bryan decided he'd listen to the music and not sing. It sounded great!

Ms. DeNard shot me a look and I started singing. Again, the music. Not the words.

EVE ARDEN

There was an actress from the 40s called Eve Arden who usually played second fiddle to the star. She had a tv show in the 50s called *Our Miss Brooks*. All this, to say that mom had a friend, Anna Brooks – and whenever I needed to refer to her, I called her 'Eve Arden'. I don't know how mom and Miss Brooks knew each other, I just always remember Miss Brooks being around from time to time.

She had an ever so slight drinking problem. *Major* slight drinking problem. And it seemed that when she needed to dry out, she'd come and stay with us from time to time, over the years. Up to the mid-80s, before she finally dried out for good. She left us and moved to Florida to a retirement village.

Miss Brooks was very funny. She had been a chorine. A dancer in her youth. Cotton Club and the like. She taught me my first dance steps.

LITTLE BRYAN STORY ALERT

"Miss Brooks, I want to do that dance where you put your knees into each other."

She showed me how that was done, and taught me the Charleston. And my first tap steps, too. I learned a lot from her. My first foreign language words – Italian, Spanish, Yiddish. She had a gentleman caller at one point, who was

German. He taught me a lullaby in German. Once again, sounds.

Because of Miss Brooks, I was introduced to the records of Moms Mabley and Red Foxx. The first time I heard Ella Fitzgerald was the album *Ella in Berlin*. A live recording. I am sure that is why I like scat singing.

My first dance lessons and a love of jazz. Thank you, Eve Arden.

SOUNDS

You know when you play that *What if?* game – "Which would you rather lose, if you had to lose one of your senses?" I'd chose to *keep* my ears. I can image sights and tastes. But I cannot cotton on to living in a world with no sound. I have no idea how Beethoven did it.

I went for a hearing test few years ago and my half-hour test lasted five minutes, and he said dogs have nothing on me. "Come back in five years."

I have always protected my ears. When I went out to a club, I'd use ear plugs. I hear and see very well from a stage. I amaze people in the audience when I say, "I heard that!"

I have always liked sounds. The ocean, rain, music, languages. I love the sound of a 747 when you first board. That hum gives me goosebumps. I live under the flight path of Heathrow Airport and when an A380 passes overhead, I *feel* that sound. The hair on my arms stands up. I've asked others, but they don't react to it.

I've been told I am good at the pronunciation of foreign words. Ella Fitzgerald and her scat singing excites me. Roz Russell in the movie *Auntie Mame,* when she spoke quickly, pleased my eight-year-old ears. Voices. Actors Richard Burton and Andrew Scott can read me their shopping list.

I suppose that is one of the reasons I chose the songs I did in my show. Rarely did it have anything to do with the words and the meaning of the songs. It was the music. The sounds. People would talk about what a song meant, and I had to go back and look at the words. I sang them, but it was the sound of the music. Music got me through Roger's illness. I would go upstairs, listen to music for twenty minutes, recharge, then head back down, ready for whatever came next. Play me a piece of music that goes from major to minor key and I can be had.

Now, do I blame Mrs. Cox for that?

THE KING AND I

There was an audition for a show being put on by a charity and to this day, I'm not sure if Ms. DeNard, the singing teacher, suggested Glenn and I go, or she mentioned it to the class. It was *The King and I.* Mom had taken us to see it in the theater, so I knew the show. I was 10 or 11, I think.

Mom dressed us up, as usual, for the audition. We sang a song and they talked to us. There were tons of kids running around the place. We were picked to be amongst the royal children.

I don't recall how long the rehearsal time was, till opening. A few months, at least. Rehearsals were after school. I was used to being in school plays all the time, but this was something much bigger.

As luck would have it, the rehearsals were in a school across the street from my grandma's home. I'd leave after my classes and go to her home until time for rehearsal to start. Perfect situation. She would feed me. Also, it made mom happier that someone was close by.

Due to my size, I was one of the larger boys in the "family". My position was in the last row. When we were on stage during rehearsal, the director was often busy with other people, and I got bored. I would sit there for a while, and then I'd shrink down, scoot underneath the back curtain, and poke my nose into other goings-on: in the prop room, the various music rooms where the principals were meeting, or the dancers practicing, etc.

Then, after a while, I would sneak back under the curtain and slowly rise back up into position again. It was my luck that a few of the young children had to be coaxed, toyed with, and had to practice many times before they got it right. Nobody even missed me. So, I did that almost every time we were on stage.

One time, I had come back to my spot and just as I was rising up – invisibly, I thought – I saw the director and conductor pointing in my direction. I thought, Oh, boy – ya done it this time, Bryan!

Mr. Hill, the director, and Mr. Boulware – whom I've been told went on to do television shows – pointed to me and said, "Can we see you after, please?"

Ok. I'm in for it now, I thought.

When rehearsal was over, I slowly walked over to them with my saddest look.

They asked me, "Can you take over the part of the crown prince?"

Would I like the part of the crown prince? In my head, I'm thinking, Do *I* think *I* could do the part of the crown prince? Were they kidding? Of course! What? I'm not in trouble for sneaking off the stage? Ok, I'll have to think for a sec…

I said to them, "YESSSSSSSSSSSSSSSSSSSSSS!"

I WAS GOING TO DO THE PART OF CROWN PRINCE CHULALONGKORN! Whoa. Talk about luck. I have no idea why they got rid of the other guy, since I had never stuck around to watch and see what he was doing. Or not.

Now, I was a principal player. This was no school play, for a change. This was big time, from my point of view.

Ben Vereen was in the production, also. I think he played the Kralahome – the Prime Minister of Siam. Nice guy to us little annoying kids. Boy, could he sing and dance.

As Prince Chulalongkorn, I got a solo to myself. Center stage. All Bryan. I had a blast doing this. It was my first time performing for a few thousand people. Yes! Nice, fancy costumes. I added several pieces of mom's jewellery. Was this the start of something?

CLASSICAL MUSIC

Who? Who? Who? Who was the next one to teach me about classical music?

Oh, what's his name? Um, err… Oh, you know him. Um. Was it Lennie something? Oh gee, why can't I recall his name. Lennie, Lennie. You'll know him when I remember his name. Wrote a couple of B'way shows. Conductor. Famous leftist. Oh. Darn. Why can't I remember him? I see his face. Leonard something. Starts with a "B". On the tip of my tongue. Leonard. Oh, yeah. Leonard Bernstein!

"What?" I hear you say. "*The* Leonard Bernstein?"

Yep. That's the one. Lennie Bernstein. My next classical music teacher. Don't be a hater. Yes – Leonard Bernstein.

"How did that come about?" I hear you asking. Well. There was a music program offered to some of the students in school. I don't recall how much it cost, but it was nothing, really. Every two weeks or so, we'd go by school bus to the Brooklyn Museum for music classes. Listening and learning classes. An introduction to classical music.

The instructor was Leonard Bernstein. I did not know who he was. He was casually dressed. No suit or tie. Open shirt. Relaxed.

He asked who liked classical music and, most of the kids being nine or ten, no one was too thrilled. He told us we already knew classical music. He played a few songs from tv shows and commercials and said they were based upon classical music. The one we all knew instantly was the theme from *The Lone Ranger*. Classical. A cereal commercial was *The 1812 Overture,* that we all knew. He was good. Made the lessons so kids could understand.

I don't recall how many times I went. I'd say it had to be at least four or five times. I will say, it was a wonderful way to get me into even more classical music.

Ok. Let's keep the haters upset, because I had great teachers.

Teachers are important.

In college, my music professor was Yusef Abdul Lateef. For those into it, he was a well-known jazz saxophone player. I didn't know who he was.

Not music but... while still on the subject of *don't be a hater and hate me 'cause I had some great and amazing teachers* – this is for the Black Studies and Women's Studies students. Poets, readers, intellectuals etc. I took a Black Studies class. Just chose it. I don't know how I got into her class, since there was a waiting list *this* long. People were standing along the sides of the room.

Professor SONIA SANCHEZ.

Sonia Sanchez is an American poet, playwright, author, speaker, educator, and activist in the Black Movement.

When Shirley MacLaine went to China in the 80s, I think it was, Sonia was part of the delegation.

When she spoke, I felt as if I were in the presence of greatness. You could hear a pin drop in the classroom. When the bell rang, no one moved. She would have to say, finally, "Ok, class is over."

All I can say is DYNAMIC. Just. Dynamic.

Teachers are important. VERY.

Enough of jealousy – back to music, now.

I mentioned to an actor friend I wanted to find a vocal coach or teacher, etc. He recommended his: Irma Jurist. I called and we met. Ms. Jurist asked what I wanted, where I was needing help.

She was a tall woman with a huge shock of red hair, which she piled high upon her head. I would have loved to have known her on a personal basis. We'd talk about the latest happenings in the world before getting down to work. I was in my last year of high school and had almost decided that classical music was not for me. I was way too much of a free spirit when it came to singing. Me and Mr. Mozart would not have gotten along, at all.

I owe my performing confidence to Ms. Jurist.

While singing, I sang the wrong note or word, and I grimaced. She stopped me and asked what was the problem? I said I made a mistake. It went like this. This is etched in my brain.

Ms. Jurist: Sing a song and make a mistake.

Me: Huh?

Ms. Jurist: Sing a song and make a mistake.

Me: I don't… um… er.

Ms. Jurist: (Getting slightly annoyed with me by now) SING A SONG AND MAKE A MISTAKE. ANY SONG. SING IT!

I sang two lines. The song, *Somewhere*. From *West Side Story*. She stopped me.

Ms. Jurist. Now, sing the same thing and make a mistake.

Me: Huh?

Ms. Jurist. Exactly. If you don't let the audience know you fucked up, they don't know.

WOW!!!!!

I studied with her for close to two years. One day, she told me she couldn't go any further with me. Nothing more to teach me. I was on my own, now. "Go out and do," she said. I had such respect for her doing that.

Talk about confidence. After that lesson, I was almost fearless on stage. Which, on one hand, is not good for me, because I tend towards being lazy about practicing. But on the other, I'm like, "Whatever". I have been known to walk on stage carrying a paper with the words to a song on it.

A good example, for me, was Ella Fitzgerald and the song, *Mack the Knife,* which she sang live in Berlin, Germany. She forgot the words and she kept on singing. The recording went on to become one of her biggest hits. After that show, she had to sing the song the same way, from then on.

NO MATTER WHAT, KEEP SINGING. Now, you understand why Amadeus would have been shooting daggers at me.

I have passed that lesson on to a few performers, and they have thanked me for it.

Thank you, Ms. Jurist.

KNOCK, KNOCK. COME OUT, COME OUT WHEREVER YOU ARE. OCTOBER 11TH

just happen to be writing this today, on National Coming Out Day. I have two major regrets in my life.

One is never coming to New York City for the first time, flying over the city or coming in by bus and looking at the city all lighted up.

And two, never having a coming out. I've never been in.

Just like the first time I picked up a crayon with my right hand and it was natural, I liked boys, not girls. It was natural. To me, hating is UNnatural.

As an adult, I can look back and see several examples of this that I did not understand as a boy, but I knew. I knew.

I can recall our baby-sitter taking me and Glenn to the movies to see what *she* wanted to see, not what we wanted. It was the film, *Tea And Sympathy*. I had no idea then what it was about but somewhere inside of me, I knew. Seven years old? When *Billy Budd* was on the television, I don't know what I knew, but I did.

My crush, if that is what you want to call it, was a young guy who lived upstairs from us. I am sure I wasn't in school yet. He told us he was an Indian, and that being the days of cowboys and Indians on tv, he had our attention. I cannot say how often, but a few times, we'd go upstairs to his place (STOP IT! HIS DOOR WAS ALWAYS OPEN!) and sit on the floor and he would tell us stories about being an Indian, on the reservation. Believe me, I would be willing to bet the ranch he was lying, but what did we know? A few minutes later, mom would call us down and tell us to stop bothering him. I have no time-frame as to how long he lived there. There was just something about him, for me. I knew. I knew.

I never had that "coming out talk" with mom. I guess she, too, just knew.

IF IN DOUBT, READ

I'm not sure when I embraced being gay or how I learned about it. Of course, there was little in print. When I went to the library, I would look for books to read about it. All were reference books and could not be taken out.

I think my education started in the mid-60s with the weekly *Village Voice* newspaper. It was an alternative newspaper. Left wing, which was where I was. It was the newspaper of Greenwich Village. The folk music scene: Dylan, Boaz, Richie Havens, et al. Anti-war. From time to time, there were articles on being gay, or gay life.

This is where I first came across the Mattachine Society – an early national gay rights organization founded in 1950 – and Dick Lietsch, the president of the New York chapter

(I learned recently that he died in 2018). I convinced Henry, my bestie, we should attend the meetings. It was thrilling to listen to men talking positively about being gay. I found this exciting. There were pamphlets to read. I was learning about me. My nascent gay life was starting. Such fun.

It was through the Mattachine Society that I met Craig Rodwell, who opened the first bookstore aimed at the gay market: The Oscar Wilde Memorial Bookshop, in 1967, in New York. Now, I could read and learn. I was still too young to go to the bars and even more so, too young to stay out past dinner time, so I had to settle for the Village Voice and these meetings.

Whenever there was an article about gay people in the newspaper or a mainstream magazine, it was never positive – or at best, just facts. Never positive. I recall an item in either *Look* or *Life* magazine about gays and the reasons why people were gay. I read it over and over and disagreed with the whole thing.

Being the pack rat that I was and still am, I kept everything I could buy or find. In the late 70s, I donated several boxes of gay clippings, papers etc. to a gay archive in New York.

My first time in a gay bar, I was 17. Julius's in the Village. Funny, if you ask many men from that time what was the first bar they went to, usually it's Julius's. It was Thanksgiving night, Thursday, November 23, 1967. Scared as hell, but my bestie dragged me there. Loved it. My people. Music from the jukebox, but no dancing.

Henry and I would go to places we'd hear about where guys hung out, and we'd make friends. Along the way, we met one guy – Fred, an actor. He was a few years older and sort of became our guardian. Our big brother. He told us things to watch out for. How to avoid trouble. Fred and I are still friends, to this day.

There were stories of police raiding the bars. The police wagon would come and haul the men to the police station. Or harass the patrons. One time, I recall hearing about a raid where a man jumped from a window and impaled himself on the spikes in the fence. Horrible. Luckily, I was never involved in a raid. The idea of mom receiving that phone call! EEK. Not being a drinker, I did not go to the bars often.

JUNE 28, 1969: STONEWALL

Freedom Day, I suppose one could say. Even though there had been another "riot" at a bar in California a couple of years before the Stonewall, the Stonewall got the better press.

One of the places Henry and I would hang out was along Christopher Street in Greenwich Village, or simply, "The Village". We'd walk along Christopher and talk with people as we headed west toward the water. I'd been in the Stonewall a few times. And the rule was, if the music stops and the lights go on, stop dancing and stand still. Fortunately for me, I never had to apply the rule.

This one night is saved to my brain, because it was the first time, the very first time in my life – my entire life – I was home alone for the weekend. All by my cute little lonesome. My brother had been accepted into Ohio State University, starting in September. He and mom had gone there to look around and to meet people. I was by myself. It was heaven. Not that I was planning a *soiree* or anything. Mind you, I could stay out late and there was no one to say anything when I would fall through the door at some ungodly hour. Or I could leave the dishes in the sink and wash them whenever.

I was with Henry at the pier when I heard all the commotion at the other end of Christopher Street. We walked a ways up the block, and then common sense hit me – not Henry. I told myself, "Bryan, get out of here and go home." I walked out of my way to get to the train home. Henry stayed.

The police seemed to like to pick on the drag queens, especially. There was a law or policy that you had to wear a couple of items belonging to your birth sex. But let's be real, no DQ of any standing was gonna wear a gown with a pair of men's brogues. Lol.

This particular night – June 28, 1969 – the police burst into the Stonewall to raid it again. But unlike other occasions, there was no prior warning, and the police became abusive and violent – inappropriately touching lesbians and demanding to verify the sex of cross-dressers. This time, the drag queens were not going to take it anymore. They refused to comply. Started throwing things at the police. This was unheard of – drag queens fighting back. But that night, they did. By the by, some of the "girls" were known to carry razor blades hidden in their bouffants. It ended up with the police barricading themselves in the Stonewall, along with a few patrons.

Outside, someone had ripped a parking meter from the ground and was using it as a battering ram to get to the police inside. Another had tried to set the place on fire. It was a night the police never forgot.

Next morning, I got up bright and early and headed back to the Village to see what had happened. Press people and police everywhere. I recall reaching about two blocks away, and seeing the tactical police marching in formation towards the Stonewall Inn. It was frightening to me.

Guys were milling around, talking. I ran into people who told me what had gone on the night before. Cars had been turned over. A police vehicle had been torched. After a while of standing on the corner of 7th Ave and Christopher Street, I headed home, where it was safe – BUT NOT ALONE! Thank you, Ohio State University.

Come Monday morning, guess whose face was plastered on the front page of the Daily News? Not mine. Henry's. Over the weekend, he had been in the thick of the protests. He was a face among the crowd. The newspapers were full of the weekend news about "Homos fighting back". The gauntlet had been thrown down. There were more disturbances, I seem to recall. Several days and nights of what the police called riots, but gays would call an uprising. Rebellion against oppression and homophobia.

It took fifty years for the NYPD to apologize for the 1969 raid.

'Stonewall' became synonymous with gay rights and liberation. Before Stonewall, the bars were owned and run by the Mafia. It was not immediate, but slowly, independent bars started to open. Windows were no longer covered up. The insides were well-lit and clean and attended to. Things were changing.

I was no longer part of the *demi monde*. It was an exciting time to be gay, from my point of view. Slowly, we were getting good press from the media. Bars and restaurants were opening. The following year, there was a gay pride march. We were still fighting tooth and nail, but bit by bit, progress was being made.

There were still cases of abuse by police and the public, but to a much lesser degree. Gay organizations were forming. The Gay Activists Alliance was one of the first that I can recall. Their headquarters was in an old fire house in the Village. Besides meetings, on Saturday night, they had dancing. It was a lot of fun. I would meet friends there and we'd dance until they threw us out at 2 AM, I believe. I loved dancing. Dance for hours.

It was during this period that I got to meet and know many of the people who would go on to be "leaders" of the gay community. And once I started working, I would be asked to do benefits and help raise money for various gay causes. A not-so-nice side to this was that whenever the check was presented to the charities, the drag queens who donated their time and talents were nowhere to be seen. Usually, you just saw the white, "straight-looking" male in the photos. Finally, a few drag queens started saying, "If we can't be on stage for the presentation, we can't be part of this". This wrong began to change.

It was a great time to be gay in New York, for me. I am aware that for many men, it was not easy to be open and out. I caught up with a friend from school that I hadn't seen in 30 years, who reminded me that I would tell anyone listening (or asking) that I was gay. He said I usually said it in Spanish. I do not recall that. I can see me doing it, though. I had no problem with it.

Others did.

One teacher in school looked as if he were direct from central casting in Hollywood: the perfect all-American college jock. I was not attracted to him in the least, but I would look at him. He took offence to this and called me out. Can you believe that? He was going to fight me because I looked at him. I said to his face, "Oh, no. Right here on school property? Kiss it good-bye. Touch me and you're done. There goes your pension." He never bothered me again.

I worked in the post office for a few months. Hated it. But the money was amazing. There was a door guard who would say things under his breath when I passed him. One day he sang the line "Fairy Tales Can Come True" from the song, *Young at Heart*. He put the emphasis on "fairy". I turned and sang back to him, the next line: "***WHEN YOU'RE YOUNG!***" That put a stop to him. *He* never bothered me again.

At the time, the fashion was for jeans to be decorated with beads, pearls, materials, all sorts of things. I had put a piece of gold brocade just below the crotch. The general manager called me to the desk and said I was not to wear those at work again. Now why did he say that to me? To quote Mr. Bugs Bunny, "*He don't know me bery well, do he?*"

You *know* the next day I wore them again. He called me to the desk and berated me for wearing them – in front of several people. I told him the regulations said nothing about wearing jeans that were decorated and secondly, "You shouldn't even be looking down there!"

And I walked away. End of him and my fashion choice. At the time, homophobia was rife in the post office. But *I* was not going to accept it.

I brought that "*DON'T FUCK WITH ME FELLAS*" (a quote from the movie *Mommie Dearest*) attitude with me across the pond to the UK.

Our homophobe MP invited some of his constituents to meet with him at the Houses of Parliament. Roger and

I went. After he did his talk, he asked for questions and comments.

Suddenly, I heard this voice that sounded just like mine – and I saw this man who looked a lot like Roger sliding under the table. (Poor Roger, I don't know how he did it. To have put up with me all those years, it had to be love).

I told the MP that I had written him about ten years ago about his anti-gay stance and asking if he had changed his opinion now. (Mind you, there were rumors about him and another MP. Said MP was later outed by an ex. So who knows?). He said he wouldn't be able to recall.

I said, "I can. Here is the letter!" I whipped it out. He was stunned.

BS. BS. BS.

He would have to look into it. He couldn't answer me. He quickly moved on – to *anyone* else. As I said – don't fuck with me, fellas…! And don't put anything in writing if you don't want me to keep it.

The late 60s into the later 70s, it was electrifying to be gay in New York. The theater scene had many gay-themed shows. *Fortune and Men's Eyes* and *Boys in the Band*, just two of them.

Let's talk about dance and disco. Every week, there was another opening of a major hot disco. My first disco was Arthur, owned by Sybil Burton, Richard's ex-wife. There was Cheetah, where I saw Sly and the Family Stone. Hippopotamus, The Loft, Paradise Garage, The Saint – to the biggie, Studio 54. I never got to Regine's. I think the first major disco was The Sanctuary. It was an old converted German Baptist church. It got a ton of press about that, which made it only more famous. This was my favorite club. I loved this place. Every Sunday, Henry and I would climb the stairs to pray to the gods of disco.

These clubs were filled with artists of every genre. Famous, not famous. Names, darling. Faces, darling. Patrons of all colors and persuasions. Several of the clubs, I would perform in, a few years later. I met and made some great friends. To walk into these places with the lights and music and the aromas was intoxicating. There was no need to partake – you got a contact high, the second you walked into the joints. My friends and I would get a limo for the evening to chauffeur us around sometimes.

MACY'S

One day, Henry said he was going to go for a job interview. I went with him. We were inseparable most of the time. He went to a department store and I sat in the waiting room while he went in. He did not get the job.

I'd never thought of working. Besides, I was still in school and the idea of work and school was far from my idea of a life.

The more I thought about it, I decided to do it. I went to Macy's instead of the store Henry went to. I figured perhaps they had a policy or reason why they did not hire him, and we were about the same in every aspect.

I did not tell anyone. I got up, and dressed in a suit. Yes, in a suit and tie. Went in and got the job. I was now a working stiff. Part-time, since I was in school. Twenty hours a week. A few hours after school and all day, Saturdays.

When I told mom, she teared up a bit. Her cute, adorable little boy, Bryan, was now old enough to work. By the by, those are my words, not hers. But she did tear up.

This was exciting. Seventeen, and making my own money now. Real money. I had had bits of jobs before. I think I was 12 years old when I started delivering the Amsterdam

Newspaper. It was a weekly aimed at the Black community. Mom knew people there and had arranged this through a friend. He would deliver the papers to us and Glenn and I went out and sought out readers. We eventually had a number of people in the neighborhood buying from us, every Thursday.

After that, we sold Christmas and all-occasion cards to our customers. All of this was great training for me on how to sell and convince people to buy. I would just knock on someone's door and sell. It was a great confidence-builder. I learned that refusal meant nothing to me.

Mom got me a Saturday job helping a man clear out the basement of his *everything in the world* store. With that money, I bought a sweater, which I had for years, and a shirt.

But now, I was in the big time. Macy's, the largest department store in the world. I was put in the stock department. I was a stock man, or as some of the older women liked to say, "stock *boy*"!

I was a flyer. Most of the men in the stock department were assigned to permanent departments, but managers would call the office for help and I'd be sent out to them. I worked over the entire store. It was great. Always somewhere different. Many of the employees knew me. I would stop and chat with people all the time.

There was one cashier around my age – Paula. I'd talk with her whenever I saw her. Ok, here it comes. Her supervisor, the relative of a famous writer, told her she should not been seen talking to me because some of the customers might not like it. Read into this what you shall. By the way, Paula was white.

One time, I was working in the men's shirt department. It was a Saturday, so, all day. I would sing the Supremes' album *Talk of the Town* to pass the time. One day, a well-dressed couple, late 50s age-wise, were passing by the counter. I remember the lady. Fully dressed, head to toe, in fur. The gentleman said they liked my singing and asked me to sing so they could hear me better. He said her name, but I had no idea who she was. For the first time in my life, suddenly I was shy. I shook my head "no". I clammed up and they walked on.

The next day, I was telling a friend what happened and described the lady. I didn't recall her name. He yelled at me, "Don't you know who that was? It was *blah, blah, blah!* She could have helped you, idiot!"

Well, I suppose I'll never know. But I don't know why I did not sing. I, who will do twenty minutes if I hear a shutter slamming, if it sounds like clapping.

Working at Macy's brought some interesting perks. I was in the Macy's Thanksgiving Day Parade two years in a row. I was *volunteered*. Perhaps a doctor's note could get you out of it, but I doubt it. All I can recall was the cold and I had to be there somewhere about 6 A.M. There was breakfast waiting for us. I got the lovely task of walking and holding down a balloon.

The first year, I was way at the end of the parade. The second year, I had Elsie, the cow balloon, at the front of the parade. It was great. By the time I got home, the parade was still going.

From Macy's – besides giving me great discounts – two romances came my way. The first one was my first boyfriend, Andy. Lasted 18 months and he *bwoke* my *liddle* heart. Just smashed it to pieces. Ahh, first love. Thankfully, Henry helped me deal with it. You must go through it to grow up. But it did not seem like it at the time.

The second was amazing. I could have loved him for a long time. However, at 19, I had not heard the phrase *bit on the side* or knew what it meant, until several years later. Sigh. But it was extremely nice. We did remain friends for several years. Just friends. Boo hoo.

All in all, I had a blast at Macy's. Well, if you look past the racist bit with Paula's supervisor and the time I got suspended for returning late after lunch. My excuse was: I got stuck on the *escalator*. Yes, I actually said that. It was the union that saved me from being fired. I've been a union man ever since that day. Big fan of unions. Then again, not all. Such as the taxi union in New York City and the union that sold out the airline, TWA. But don't get me started.

With my singing teacher, Ms. Jurist, setting me free, and the break-up of my young love romance, I started thinking it was time to go off out into the world. I left Macy's. I would miss the people and the discounts, but not getting up before the sun on Thanksgiving morning, and putting on my long drawers and 19 layers of clothing to march down Broadway. I gave notice, the beginning of September. Two weeks later, I was doing community theatre, performing in schools. I was getting paid a pittance, but I was a working actor. Welcome to show business, Bryan.

It was through the trades, I got the job with the repertory theater company. I went for the audition. This was the first time I had auditioned. I hadn't learned about picking the correct audition pieces to use, yet.

Now you *wanna* hear about having big brass ones? I used the opening to *I'm the Greatest Star* from *Funny Girl*. Diana Ross' version. Oh, yes, I did. Speaking it. They hired me. I think they just could not get over my gall, nerve, guts. But I did it.

We met, four days a week. My travel time was over an hour and my start time was 10:00 A.M. In the morning! A.M.! I was still singing at the showcases at night, around town, also. We performed in the schools around the city. It was silly stories and funny costumes and a lot of noise and movement. One of my fellow actors was Dennis Dugan who went on to do movies, theater, comedy, and direct.

I started with the company in September, and they fired me in December. It was my travelling time that did it. I was never late for a performance, just the days we would study and have acting classes. I wasn't very upset. I hated doing the shows for the brats. And it would not be the last time I got fired from a show. Ahh, show biz. A week later, I got the play, **Sweet Tom**.

From every cursing comes a blessing, mom used to say. Right at that moment, I could not disagree.

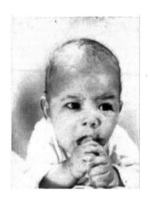

AWWWWWWWWWWW. Such a cutie.

They told me, I ran out of the house and straight to the pony.

Christmas morning. Me and Glenn.

Me and my brother, Glenn.

Madame Taylor would not approve of those hands.

Mom and me

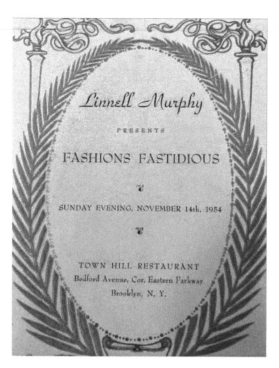

Program from a show of mom's.

Mom in one of her designs.

Conducting the chorus for a school play.

I'm a working actor. Even if it is for kids.

ACT II

WELCOME TO THE NAKED 70S

New York was fantastic around that time. There was so much going on, artistically. The swinging 60s led to the sexy 70s. There were plays with nudity. *Hair* was 1967 and the most famous one, I believe. *Oh, Calcutta*, and throw in a few others. Then, add the play I was in.

Huh?

Yep. *Nekkid*. It was a job. I will say, though, I think every actor should do a nude play. After the first few performances, you won't care about much. If I thought I had confidence before, I certainly did after the run of the play. All very exciting. We ran for about three months. I had a blast. I was doing theater. I was an actor.

During this time, I was singing in the cabarets around town. Doing my two or three numbers. Learning my trade.

As much fun as I was having, one needed money to eat and buy clothes. Yes, once upon a time, I dressed fashionably. One time in school, a kid passed me a note and asked how many pairs of shoes did I have? My reply was, "I don't know". I didn't. I rarely wore the same thing twice in two or three weeks. Then, of course, you needed going out clothes. And money to go follow the Supremes, eat in good restaurants and limo to the clubs.

BRYAN WORKS.
BRYAN GETS A JOB.

Yeah, I know. Shocking. It was during this time, after I finished the play, I decided to find employment.

I did what a lot of actors did: I signed with an agency that would work around a performer's schedule. I did various one- or two-day office jobs. That did not work out very well, since they wanted me there at 9 A.M.

I got a job at Rockefeller Center. I loved being in that building. I learned about the tunnels connecting the buildings in the area. At one time, you could walk from 6th Avenue and 55th Street all the way to 30th Street and 8th Avenue, underground. A friend called me "mole man". But it was handy on rainy or snowy days.

The 9 A.M. was killing me and the supervisor let me go. No one seemed to understand – I don't do 9 A.M. Unless it was from the night before. Which happened rather often.

Then I hit paydirt. Sorta. Again, the 9 A.M. thing, but it was fun. And only one train, for me. So, I gave it a go. For me, the other workers were good. One of the actors was Wesley Eure. He went to do a soap on telly and now is – or was – the husband or boyfriend of Richard Chamberlain.

I was still not doing well with the time. One day, the boss, whom I loved, asked me if I could get in at nine. I figured, ok – this is it, Bryan, and I said, "No. It's too early."

Then, we started playing a game. "Can you do 10?" she asked.

"No."

"11? Can you do that, Bryan?"

By now, I'm going for it. "I can get here by 12 – and that's a promise."

Knock me over with a feather boa, she said "Fine". She would make me part-time and get someone else to come in, in the mornings. Wow. No idea why she did that, but she did. And I was never late again.

MISS. PEARL BAILEY

There was a tv show, *The Ed Sullivan Show*. Every Sunday night. A musical variety show. It was there that I saw all types of performers. One of my favourites was Pearl Bailey. She would come out and destroy that fourth wall you hear actors talk about. Ms. Bailey would head for the audience. She would take over the theater. I loved how she took control and was in command.

When she starred in *Hello Dolly* on Broadway, I saw the show 13 times. You could get a seat way up in the nosebleed section for $5. I studied her. Watched her. I learned from her how to work a stage and an audience. When things went wrong on stage, it did not faze her. She could deal with it. And ad-lib – wow. Whatever it was, Ms. Bailey was ready. For example, the time her co-star split his pants and had to run off and change. Or when Carol Channing came to see her and got on stage to sing with her and one of the mics was not working. Pearl had the audience in stitches. I bought the cast album and would listen to it and act out Pearl's dancing and sing along with the record.

I had seen my first drag show and wasn't terribly impressed. You had a Diana Ross or a Shirley Bassey, or a few other female stars. No one was singing. Just moving their lips and not very well, at that. I always thought I could do better – plus, I'd be singing. Friends talked me into auditioning for the club – *doing* Pearl Bailey.

The club was beautiful. It was a real night club. My type of place. Classy. I went in for the audition. If the audience liked you, you'd get to do 2 shows a night, two times, two weeks in a row. Nervous as hell. I think it was to do two numbers. I did it and got not one, but two standing ovations before I was through, and left the stage while they were asking for more. Everyone concerned – except the drag queen in charge, who was not happy – said they loved me.

I did get the gig, though. I put together my little show with comedy and audience participation and songs. I was a hit. I had a full night club routine. And the money was more in the one night than I was making a week as an office temp.

My nascent show biz career was born.

Next, I needed costumes, hair, make-up and shoes. Yes, lady's shoes to fit my gun boats.

One time, I was sitting in a lady's shoe store. A little boy was watching me try on the shoes. He asked his mother why that man was wearing lady's shoes. She said, "Just sit down and be quiet.!

After my successful shows at the club, I got auditions for some other clubs; then, once I started working, I no longer had to audition. I got the gigs. I was learning new Pearl Bailey songs non-stop.

The work was coming in from around the city. Then, a few from the outer boroughs. I was enjoying developing my new act.

ONE FROM COLUMN A AND I'LL HAVE AN EGG ROLL AND FRIED RICE, TOO

I was working in a club in New Jersey, right across the water from Manhattan – my first "out of town" gig. A man named Frank came up to me after the show, saying he was the manager of a bar on the Upper West Side called the Westside, and he'd be interested in talking to me. Sure.

A week or so later, I showed up, bringing my Chinese food lunch with me. As he and his cast members were rehearsing, I sat in the back row, blissfully eating my lunch. One day sometime later, Frank said he just admired me for showing up and sitting in the back with my food. He couldn't believe anyone would do that.

This began the growth period for my career. I was hired to do one night a week. That lasted for over two years. During that time, I joined their show cast in their shows. I learned how to work an audience. My ad-libbing developed. I learned how to think on my feet. This was my training ground. I also decided to add Tina Turner to my repertoire. I got two friends and we put together a Tina Turner and the Ikettes show. No singing this time. Just lip sync and dancing non-stop. No one could touch me when it came to performing. Pearl or Tina. The feedback was beyond great. I/we got write-ups and reviews. It was good.

My area was widening. Firstly, I wanted to do the five boroughs, then Atlantic City, and Asbury Park, New Jersey. I set my sights on Connecticut. Throw in the clubs on Long Island.

It was during this period at the Westside where I met one of the major influences on me and my career. Bobby Kneeland. Bobby was the sound and lighting tech person for the Westside. We were friends from 1972 till his death in 2013. I learned about sound and lights. In the beginning, I wanted to be the star, of course. Bobby explained how Marlene Dietrich knew as much about lighting and sound as – or maybe even more than – the theatre tech people.

Always be nice to your tech people. They are the ones

who will make you look and sound good. I never forgot that. During my shows, I would graciously thank my techies from the stage.

I would travel with gels for lights. My own mic and cords. When I arrived at a club, I'd have the lights rearranged. Turn speakers away from me to prevent feedback. I like to think that some of the clubs learned, from me, how a show should be presented. Or I tried. Often, I was met with resentment. They would proudly hand me a mic from a home sound system and wonder why I did not think it was good. Ha! Or put me in a light with a green or red coloured gel and say how good I looked. It was Bobby who taught me to always leave a dressing room better than I found it. Which sadly, was not difficult. One club I worked at in Chicago, the owner called her staff to come and see how I cleaned up after myself. She said no one ever cleaned up before they left.

Bobby set up the stage lights and sound for many of the cabaret rooms in Manhattan. I would go along as his assistant. It was at one club, the Finale Night club, where I got to know and do tech for people such as Nina, Chita, Nancy, Sarah – no last names needed. (Ok. If I must: Simone, Rivera, Wilson, Vaughan). And many more. It was at the Finale that Sarah and I became friends and she invited me to stay at her home when I was in LA. She was working a club for a week and every night I was able to watch her. I got to see how greatness worked. And I learned that some club owners tried to do as little as possible, dressing room-wise, to make an artist comfortable – even at her level. Sad, really.

WEREN'T YOU RECENTLY ON THE DAVID SUSSKIND SHOW?

In the early 70s, drag was getting bigger. There were clubs and theater shows with drag queens. It was becoming mainstream. I appeared on the David Susskind TV Show. Me and five other drag performers, talking about drag. You had Mae West, Diana Ross, Bette Midler, Marlene Dietrich, and me – Pearl Bailey. Since the show was being taped, they wanted us to first be ourselves, then change quickly and be the performer. This was my first time on tv as a performer. Fun.

I ran into my first boyfriend. We hadn't seen each other in five years. I puffed up and asked if he'd seen me on the tv and was he surprised? He said yes, and no, he wasn't surprised, since this was what I had said I wanted to do. There, went the wind out of that sail, for me. On one hand, great compliment; on the other, no bragging there, or "See what you missed?"

I was working a lot and having a blast. Everything was going great, career-wise. The love life, not so good. I dated, here and there. Never meeting anyone when I was working. Working at night in clubs doesn't leave much time for dating someone who probably worked during the day.

That was about to change. A gent came up and asked if I'd been on the David Susskind Show recently. I smiled and said yes. And that was that. His name was Ernie and this was 1974. He became my first real boyfriend in a long-term relationship. Fourteen years. A nice man, but for one major problem. His drinking. Sadly. I always said we should have broken up after ten years. But considering AIDS was coming down the pike in 1982, I'm glad we didn't. I suppose I can say that he probably saved my life.

A problem for a lot of club performers is – it is work for us, but to others, it is fun time. Drinking time. In the beginning of our relationship, Ernie would travel with me sometimes. Especially when I was working out of town. Weekend away. Hotel time. I noticed that once he would take advantage of the owners' offer to have drinks, he could not say no. I knew of some entertainers who had partners who drank too much and I knew how they were talked about – not in a nice way. There was no way this was going to happen to me. Consequently, I would leave him home when I worked. Perhaps a couple of times a year, I'd bring him with me if it was a fun location, but when I went to work, I'd leave him in the hotel.

There was never any big drama or anything like that. I was watching him spiral downwards with his booze and I was not going with him. When I got to the *I'm not taking this any longer* point, I confronted him and he told me he didn't have a problem with his drinking – *I* had a problem with it.

I gave him a choice: of finding a solution about his drinking – or me. I was prepared for his answer. We split, December of 1988. Fourteen and half years and I was fine about it. He did try, but once a drug gets a hold of someone, it is difficult to fight it.

IT'S NOTHING PERSONAL BUT...!

The mid to late 70s were getting better and better for me. Besides a new love, I got two fantastic opportunities.

Bobby Kneeland, besides setting up sound and lighting in clubs, also did theater lighting and sound. I had worked with him on a few around the New York area, but he now was working at a theater outside of Washington, D.C. in Arlington, Virginia.

He invited me down to see what he was doing, and to see the show. He had told them about my show and suggested that I perform while I was there. Me? On a real theater stage? In front of actors? Oh gee, I guess I could be persuaded. GRIN.

They did an early show on Sundays. A few select invites went out to people and the cast stayed afterwards. My performance was alive. I was on fire. Theater folk. They got everything I did. Understood every move I made. Every nuance. I loved it. I probably did about an hour and half. A good time was had by all. Especially me – and Bobby, being proud of his friend.

After a weekend there and saying my goodbyes and thanks, I left for home.

Bobby called me several weeks later. One of the people who had been invited to see me had written a play called *Laughing Gas* – about Samuel Colt, the inventor of the revolving gun, who taught dentists to use laughing gas (nitrous oxide). He thought I would be perfect for one of the parts. Starring role of Saint Apollonia, the Patron Saint of Dentists. Huh? What? Who? I was sent the script and said ok. A six-week run. Two-week rehearsal and then, on stage. I hadn't done a play in a number of years. All of the details worked out. I was happy.

OH BOY, SOMETHING IS NOT RIGHT, HERE.

The weekend before I was to leave, I was working a resort on Long Island, New York. Great place. I loved working there. Right on Long Island Sound. They had a pool. Me and a pool! I jumped into the water and after about *ten minutes* on the bottom of it, something in my brain said, Bryan, something is not right, here. Long story short. In pain. Friends drove me back to the city. I went to the hospital the next day.

Doctor: A one in a million chance. You chipped a bone in your knee. I'll admit you to the hospital.

Me: You can't admit me to the hospital.

Doctor: Why not?

Me: I have to be in Virginia in three days.

Doctor: Then put we'll put a cast on it.

Me: Ok. If you have to.

Annoyed. I had a cast on my leg from thigh to ankle. Not happy.

I call Bobby and tell him. He gets back to me, after discussing it with the powers that be. They say they'll write it into the script. My part is such that it won't matter.

Yippee. Off to Virginia I go. A friend drives me down, since no way could I drive.

Now may I tell you, the director, Ardith, was a terror. Maniacal. Hell in high heels. Beelzebub incarnate. I saw her actually trip her husband as he was passing her because she was angry at him. Mean to everyone but me. For some reason, she never "voiced" annoyance to, or with, me. Ardith would curse, scream, or throw things at actors if she wasn't happy about something they did or didn't do. Again, not me. It was to come.

The playwright and Ardith worked my cast into the play and allowed me to loosely do my dialogue, as long as I made sure I gave the actors their cue lines. At times, I could hear the actors stifling laughter at something I said. I loved this. This was my dream.

There was one actor. Method. My style made him nuts. He made Ardith crazy. He got most of her bile. He needed to know his motivation for every single tiny little thing. Her usual response to his "Why am I doing this?" was "Because I'm paying you."

He did corner me once and questioned me as to what caused me to do what I do. I wanted to yell and scream and throttle him myself. I once worked with another method actor and we spent 15 minutes on the first 45 seconds of the show!!!!!

We'd been in previews for a week or so, when one evening, I had left early to go back to the house where everyone was staying. Bobby came in later and was acting strangely. I asked him what was what. He looked crestfallen.

I said, "She's firing me – right?" I knew. She said my part was just not working out. She never had the balls to tell me. I never saw her again.

Bobby was upset. Fine with me. I'd get back home to Ernie six weeks sooner. I flew home.

Later that week, a local news rag came out with a review of the show. Bobby called and read it to me. I will always remember this: ***"THE ACTING WAS NOT PARTICULARLY NOTEWORTHY WITH THE EXCEPTION OF THE YOUNG STAND-UP COMEDIAN, BRYAN MURPHY."***

Bobby said she was evil as a wet hen for the next few days and never said a word to anyone about the review. And you know, the funny thing is, as sadistic, vicious, and brutal as she was, I'd work with her in a second. I loved her as a director. Perfect for me.

DON'T BOTHER ME,
I CAN'T COPE

In 1976, I got a call from the office of the Broadway producer, Norman Kean. He was producing a show in Washington, D.C., featuring a female singer and five or six drag queens. The concept of the show was strange to me, but what did I know? Norman was the famous Broadway Producer. His big show was *Oh! Calcutta!*, the naked show that he kept running for ages. Also, he produced a favourite show of mine, *Don't Bother Me, I Can't Cope*. Love the music from that show.

It was going to be in the show room of a big hotel. A two-month contract, I seem to recall. Everything in order. Contracts signed, retainer fee paid. Yea.

Week later, Norman's office calls. "Mr. Kean would like to see you."

I get there. Sad look on his face. He is cutting me. And why? Ready?

Because there would be too many Black performers in the show. HUH? And, to an audience, a Diana Ross trumps a Pearl Bailey in popularity. Nothing for me to say. He buys me out of my contract. The hurt and pain did not last long once that check cleared. Believe me.

Ahh, show biz. Don't bother me – I CAN cope if the buyout is that good.

I never heard how the show went. I did hear about the

sad and tragic ending of Norman Kean. Murder/suicide in 1988. Horrible.

WHY ARE YOU A PERFORMER?

Depending upon the venue, one of my favorite parts of my show is when I would throw the floor open to questions, comments, statements, or requests. I called this my hand-to-hand combat section of the show. If I were at a large club, or in a theatre setting, there was no way to do that. However, in a sit-down night club type of place, I would do it. I always figured I could work out a response one way or another. Usually, I went for the joke. Sometimes, it was to sing a song. Generally, I would sing it acapella. Didn't bother me. I'd go for it. Sometimes just a line or two. It would depend upon the song. Or there were times I'd do the entire song, if possible. I might even have the music on a disc with me.

When the club had a host, I would give the host index cards and have them tell the audience to write anything on the cards. That was so much better, and much more fun. This way they didn't have to be embarrassed or shy. They could ask anything – and trust me, they did. I would never look at the cards until they were handed to me on stage. This way, I would be surprised and challenge myself to think quickly on my feet.

"What is your favorite sexual position?"

Me: Standing… in line at the bank, making a withdrawal.

"When was the last time you had sex?" or "What was the best sex you ever had"?
Me: Five minutes after you left the room.
"Would you have sex with me?"
Me: How much money do you have?
"Is there anything you won't do?"
Me. Yeah. You!
"Are you a boy or a girl?"
Me: No, I'm a democrat.

It didn't matter, I was game. And sometimes, the questions would cross over the line. Did not bother me – I'd read it out loud and answer it. Only, if it was nasty or hurtful about someone in the room, I would not read it aloud. I'd make some joke comment about it being written in crayon and to "Get that 5-year-old out of the room and back in his bed. He has school in the morning." Or some such.

Now you wanna know if I was ever stumped by a question? YES! ONCE. Only once.

Ready for the question? I'm sure you're thinking it was something dirty or sexual. Nope.

Ok, here it is: "Why are you a performer?"

Me: ...

Struck silent. No answer. Can you believe that question stopped me cold? I had no answer. None.

Disappointed? I was, also. I'd never been unable to come

up with something to say. I honestly do not recall what I said to that.

But while we're on the subject, what do you think I had wanted to be/do – if not an entertainer?

No. You're wrong.

I would love to have been an airplane pilot. I could not do cabin crew. My Brooklyn would come out and I'd be fired the first day. I love aeroplanes. Love them. Love them. I love to fly. When it was announced that the Concord was on its last legs, I thought of booking a flight before they were grounded for good. I went back and forth. Do it. Spend the money. Or don't, and save my relationship with Roger. It was close, but he won out. Probably 51% to 49%. He would have gone ballistic if I spent that much. He will never know how close he came.

Or a spy for a country. Seems exciting. And who would ever suspect cute little old me of trading government secrets?

Or an archaeologist. That would be fun. Going on digs, discovering and touching things that had not been seen in thousands of years. But not in the hot sun and sand. Not my thing. One time when I was in Egypt, there was a lot of excitement. They had uncovered something, right at that moment. That was exciting for me.

Or a computer nerd. I'd be a computer hacker. That would be interesting.

A motivational speaker perhaps? I do know I am good at motivating people.

I still don't have an answer to why I was a performer. Just a calling. Something I had to do I suppose.

COME FLY WITH ME, LET'S FLY, LET'S FLY AWAY

November 1977, things really started moving for me. I had started setting goals and setting my sights on places I wanted to work. I had a fully developed night club act. I was all over the New York tri-state area and down to the Carolinas. Anywhere that was a day's car-drive away.

I had put together a resume and press kit, and it was impressive. One owner even said his tablecloths were not as good a quality as the paper I was using in my kit.

A friend had moved to Florida and suggested I get in touch with one of the big clubs there. I sent off my package. They called and wanted to book me and would fly me down. They booked a tour around the state that lasted for a week or so. That was it. That was the beginning of *HAVE DRAG WILL TRAVEL* – by plane, car, boat, train, bus, skateboard, or anything moving down the highway. Now, my plans were set on anywhere there was an airport.

The timing was good, 'cause my friend Glenn was working all over and I could catch up with him in places. And brother, did we. All around the globe. Europe, Australia, and the states.

One time, I was invited to join Village People for dinner

at a night club in Paris. Glenn left early. Alex and I stayed till late.

As we were walking the streets of Paris back to our hotel at 2 A.M., it dawned on me – "This is the life I planned". This was another of my teenage dreams coming true. Meeting fellow entertainers around the world.

WORK

As time went on, I dropped Pearl from my show. Instead of singing over the recording of her voice, I had a machine that could eliminate her voice, and it was more me. I would add songs that I liked. Show tunes of course (I am gay, you know). A few "hits" from the radio. And a lot of songs that I call "Bryan songs". Comedy songs.

One of my favourites is *Living Next Door To Alice*. Roger and I were walking in a town up north in England. I heard this playing from a music store. I stopped and said to him, "What is that? I must have that. I gotta do that song."

The version I heard was by the band, Smokie, from 1977. In 1995, a Dutch band, Gompie, produced a ruder version. In my show, it's an audience participation song. Their part is "Alice, Alice – who the fuck is Alice?!!" Go and Google it. There have been a few times I've been asked to do the song again. It is certainly a people pleaser.

Amazingly, I have been hired quite often because I do

not curse on stage. I do a clean show. Whenever someone said that to me, I had to chuckle to myself. 'Cause off stage, that certainly ain't the case.

I'd do songs by Shirley Bassey, Tina, Diana, Sarah. Whatever made me happy. Glenn once accused me of doing the shows for my own pleasure. I couldn't totally argue with him.

I even went way back to my roots. Classical music. I would end the show with a classical piece. One was *Jesu, Joy Of Man's Desiring* by Bach. But being Bryan, I scatted it. Then, the killer was Puccini's *Nessun Dorma* from Turandot. That one, I did straight… (Well…!). At the end, when I went for that last note, I would see who in the audience was wincing, waiting for me to fail. I would sing the note perfectly, stick my tongue out at him; then, hit the note again just to show off.

Sometimes I was booked for a weekend. Two or three nights. I would join the house cast of several artists. The performers would lip sync one or two numbers, then another cast member would go on. The host would tell me how many numbers I could do, since I was the star of the show. Because I was live and not lip syncing, I would tell them, "Don't give me numbers, tell me how much time you want me to do."

I think the longest show I ever did was in Baltimore. I was on stage over two hours and fifteen minutes. Kathy was not a happy bunny that night. They wanted more, but I said to myself, finally, "Enough, Bryan. Get off. Go eat and then, back to the hotel and go to sleep."

WEARING A DRESS

Drag Race and *Pose*, amongst other shows, have put drag center-stage. This is good. The last 10 years or so, drag has become popular, thanks to RuPaul and Ryan Murphy.

In the early 2000s, I had a meeting at BBC Television Centre at White City, London, with Jon Plowman, the film and television producer. For the life of me, I do not recall how I got the gig, but I had to go into the meeting dressed. I must say, I did look fantastic, and talked about drag with Jon and maybe ten more people. They wanted my input on why drag was starting to grow. What was the interest?

I answered their questions and responded to the comments. I told them I was an actor and drag was just a show. A uniform. A costume. Nothing more.

When it comes to drag in the US, I would be willing to say that more than half of the performers are into drag as a lifestyle. Good for them, I say. But for me, it's way too much work. And I hate, with a passion, shaving. I put drag on and take it off as soon as possible. Often, I was asked why I didn't use a female name, as most do. Why? I like my name and I'm not female. I think I puzzled a lot of the girls. I worked in one drag bar and the owner, who was a drag queen, was annoyed with me because after the show, I didn't walk around the joint, still dressed. I had changed back into my Bryan clothes.

In New York, I knew many of the "girls" the actors are portraying in Pose. And the reality is a million times worse than you see in the tv show. In the documentary movie, *Paris Is Burning* (1990), again, I knew many of the people in that. In fact, Miss Dorian did an outfit for me. She became infamous after she died, when a body that had been there for twenty years or so was found in her home.

BLIGHTY

When I got to the UK, I had to tweak my show a bit. Here, most of the entertainers sang live. I was thrilled. More comedy was added to the show. Once again, I was different. I could base my humor on being a Yank in the UK.

There were a number of gay comedy clubs opening up. I started doing stand-up. That was a lot of fun for me. Maybe I'd do one funny song, but the rest was comedy. No music to fall back on. Nothing was written. I'd go on and just go for it. Most of it off the top of my head.

Now comes the bad part. Sadly. In the US, as well as the UK, some people were bad-mouthing me. But that's ok. It goes with the territory. I don't understand that. Jealousy. There is room for everyone. I could do a **BROOKLYN** response to them here, but instead, I'll go the nice route – to quote Maya Angelou, ***STILL I RISE***.

MEMORABLE NIGHTS

There have been many highlights for me, working. Here, I'll just mention a few. They were un-friggin' believable.

In New York, every June, for Gay Pride, I'd entertain. When I saw Lena Horne's show, I was excited by her entrance. The overture and no announcement – she simply walked on and started singing. I loved that.

That year at the pride show, I told the host, "Don't introduce me," as he had done with the others. I was going to push my luck and see how well-known I was to the New York crowd. My turn came, and as I walked up the stairs to the stage, I could hear the applause and cheering as they could see me, as I rose. Fantastic!!!!

I was part of a show at a big club in New York. I was given my time slot. The place had a staircase to come from the dressing room to the stage. Oh, lordy, be still my beating heart. Me on a staircase. YES! My plan was to walk down to the music, stop it, talk about my love of the staircase etc., turn around and go back up, then come down again. The producers were not happy with my plan. All the reasons that it might not work, they came back to me with. I said it would work.

Show night. DAMN. It was great. Worked better than even I thought. Later that evening, the producer was man enough to say how pleased they were, and that I was right. I thanked them.

There was a benefit to raise money for The Gay Softball League of New York. I was one of many people asked to entertain. I was allotted fifteen minutes. As if! Get the hook.

There were teams from all over the US, and Canada, too. And when I was finished, the cheering and shouting and applause was deafening. That was a first. I understood what noise torture was all about, then. It was piercing. My entire body shook. It hurt my ears. But the money was pouring in as I sang and joked.

Lastly. In San Jose, Costa Rica, I did my show in English and Spanish. They loved me. Do you hear? Loved me. LOVED ME! Yell, scream, shout. They did it all – and more. They'd never seen anyone like me.

Not a night, but oh, so memorable – I met Leonard Matlovich. He was a decorated soldier who challenged the military's policy of removing gay people. This was backstage of the bandshell in Central Park, in New York. Before the route for the gay march was changed, it used to start in the Village and end in the park. I had been scheduled to perform, but everything was delayed, and Matlovich was the main speaker. I did enjoy meeting and talking with him.

When he died, he'd had written on his tombstone: "*When I was in the military, they gave me a medal for killing two men and a discharge for loving one.*"

NOT SO...

If you don't know me, I tend to talk a little. Or as Roger said, I don't know the meaning of brevity.

You know there are those times when you want the ground to open up and swallow you? Either Mothman or Rodan should swoop down, grab you and take you away?

Well. One time, I was asking people in the audience what they wanted for Christmas. I'd put the mic in their face and say, "Tell me. Tell me. What do you want for Christmas?"

I got to one woman and asked her. I would not shut the frig up. She fumbled with her pocketbook. And did Bryan stop? You bet he didn't. I said, "Yes, yes. That's it. Put your glasses on. Look at me. What do you want for Christmas?" (Even now, I'm breaking out in a sweat). "What do you want?" Mic in her face. (Kill me now, lord. Just kill me where I stand).

"I want Jesus Christ to give me back my eyesight."

OUCH.

Because I tend to hear and see well on stage, when I want people to clap, I can usually hear if someone is clapping on 1 & 3 beats. Off beat. So, I go over to them, take their hands and get them started clapping *on* the beat. And if I see someone is NOT clapping, I will yell at them to clap. NOW, YOU KNOW WHAT IS COMING – RIGHT?

Not one, but two different shows, I went up to someone

who was not clapping and yelled at them to clap and they only had one arm.

You know, there are those times when I wished I had become a monk. Ahh, show biz.

MY FUN

I live for hecklers. They bring me such joy. I love it when they start with me, and I get to lay them out like lavender whale shit. One would think people would learn. But nope. Never start on the comedian with a microphone. Chances are you're gonna lose. I'm a black belt responder. Peel, pare and cut them before they've taken a breath.

I did a tv show in the UK. This was interesting for two reasons. I did the show in drag. I had one request for the producers: my dressing room had to have a/c. My face melts fast if I'm waiting around. I don't mind if I sweat on stage, but at least let me arrive looking "pretty".

They kept me hanging around for a few hours till I was needed. As my time came closer, the interns would come in and try to get me hyper about possible comments the audience might make about me, since I was the only one dragged up. My comment was, "I'll be fine."

Later, another one would come and crank it up a bit. "If they say 'blah, blah' what will you say?" On and on. And I coolly responded, "I'll be fine."

I wasn't getting all up in arms enough for them. Then,

the big boss came in and tried his best to get me roiled up. Again: "I'll be fine".

My time. I hit the stage, and a guy started with me. I sliced and diced, and he sat down, tail between his legs – and not another peep out of him. Or anyone else to me, for that matter. Others on stage, but not to me. The audience loved it.

In the green room after the taping, the participants in the show were all arguing, threatening to call lawyers, hating how they came off. Not me. The big guy came over to me and my friend who went with me, while we were outside the room eating our food, and said how good I came across and he had thought *I* was going to be the problem. I said, "I told y'all I'd be fine." Score one for the DQ from Brooklyn.

I will say, I do not know how I think of these things, but they come into my head in a millisecond, then out of my mouth. I even surprise myself, sometimes. My favourite one is this. A heckler yelled that he was a god, and I said, "You're dyslexic!"

The audience was on the floor. Where did that come from? No thinking, just responding. It's a gift – and I accept it and cherish that ability.

I do have such fun, if I say so myself. So perhaps Glenn was correct. I do shows for my enjoyment.

GOOD-BYE. YOU ARE THE...

I was working in Bristol, England, with several other acts. Someone mentioned that there was going to be a Drag Queen version of the Weakest Link and there were people going around to the clubs to look for drag participants.

Lo and behold, they came to see the show where I was working. After the show, they came to the dressing room and spoke with some of us. I have no idea what their criteria were, or what they had in mind. My turn, they asked a few general knowledge questions. I answered to the best of my ability. The one question I recall answering before anyone else was: "What does OFT stand for?"

I don't know why I knew that right away, but I yelled, "Office of Fair Trade!" Then, they took names and details.

I get a call to come and be on *The Weakest Link*. It was fun and I lasted a long time before being voted off.

We must have had great ratings, because there was a second time on the show. Ann Robinson was fun. I enjoyed both times.

ON THE ROAD AGAIN. AGAIN. AGAIN. AND AGAIN

As much as I was enjoying the work, my enthusiasm for traveling probably matched it. I have been to 48 states of the United States and performed in forty-three of them. As I say, I'm sure I've seen almost as many hotels as a $2 working girl, but mine are 5-star hotels. I love the excitement of a new city. The people and the food.

My number one favorite, without a doubt, is New Orleans. The food. I'd get off the plane, check in, hit Jackson Square and try to eat my way around the area. I'm a big history buff and New Orleans has amazing history. That would be followed closely by Charleston, South Carolina. Great history – and the she-crab soup? Yes, yes, yes. I am also willing to bet that, at one time, I knew every Dunkin' Donuts location off of highway I-95 from New York to South Florida.

Driving was my relaxation. Leaving right after a show and heading to the next venue at 2 A.M. was enjoyable. Roads were empty. I had my CB radio and would listen to the truckers chatting back and forth. They would signal to one another where the smokies (highway patrols) were. I needed to know that, too. I'm a pedal to the metal driver. What speed limit?

My best time was leaving San Diego on the west coast of America on Monday evening after rush hour and pulling into Towson, Maryland, on the east coast of America on

Friday afternoon for a show, Saturday. The longest tour I did was twenty-two days, with eighteen shows in different locations. Several states. After that one, I made myself a promise – never again. Too much by myself. I loved the driving, though.

Whenever I left home to go driving around the country, mom would always say, "Stop by and say hello to…" aunt, cousin, brother, mother, sister, uncle, grandpa, stranger.

And I would say, "Yeah, mom, sure. Ok. Right."

I never did. She always said our family was big. I did not care. I didn't know these people and I wanted to keep it that way.

Fast forward almost 20 years. I knew we had a family historian in the family – Sam, who has traced the family back to 1806. He and I were email friends for a long time. A cousin had convinced me we should travel to North Carolina and see Sam and the family. She knew them from past trips. Sadly, we never did. She died two years after Roger.

I finally said, life is short, Bryan. Do it. WELL. Mom. I underestimated or misunderstood what she meant by a "big family". It's rare that I am speechless. THAT FAMILY IS HUGE. HUGE. HUGE. Do you hear what I say? HUGE.

I was only in town for two days and it was non-stop family and family history. There is a school named after a relative. One was a politician and has a park named after him. Street, cemetery, neighborhood. HUGE. There's one cousin I wish I could have spent more time with. She went to the Sorbonne in Paris during the turbulent 60s. Now, she would have *great* stories. I was stunned.

I *shoulda* listened to mom, but oh, well.

Sadly, there is a downside to all my driving. It is **D.W.B**.

DRIVING WHILE BLACK

Oh, yeah. I was "profiled" more than 30 times. And only once did I get a ticket. I was speeding and couldn't argue that one. I think twenty of those times was in the state of New Jersey. And it was always the same. Did I have firearms, drugs, booze, cigarettes? Stop. Search. Check.

The reasons were always one of these. Going too slow. Going too fast. Wrong lane. Couldn't see my plate. Looked as if I were weaving in the lane. Rear of the car was hanging low to the ground.

And since we're on the unpleasant subject –

(FILL IN THE BLANK) … **WHILE BLACK**

LEARNING...

I was in second grade. Every day, we'd have cookies and milk, mid-morning. I believe the cost was two cents for the two cookies. Some of the students would place the money on the desktop.

Two times, a girl said her money was missing. The assistant principal was called. Both times, I was called out of the room and taken in back of the staircase, where he searched my pockets and even had me take my shoes and socks off. No money was found, because I hadn't taken it. This happened to me two times. Oh, by the way, I was the only black kid in the class. I have no idea why I never told mom, but I didn't.

COMPLIMENTED...

It was the summer between elementary and middle school. My brother and I were invited for lunch by my last teacher and his present teacher. During the visit, after looking us over, one of them said she would feel safe if we were walking in back of her at night. Meaning – the way we looked, we did not appear as threatening to her as some young Black boys might. I was 12 and not yet capable of knowing how best to respond. So I said nothing, but this time I did tell my mother. For the life of me, I do not recall what she said.

Growing up, I'd get the "You speak so well…!" *compliment* and other back-handed compliments pertaining to my skin color.

SHOPPING...

I cannot even tell you the number of times I've been followed while shopping. One time, in Bergdorf's in New York, the guard **wasthisclosetome**. So, I turned and asked him if he thought the sweater I was interested in would fit me. I went to the desk and asked for the manager.

When she came out, I said, "It's very disconcerting trying to shop while he is following me." And I put the sweater down and walked out.

Sometimes, when I have time and am in a fun mood, I'll play with them. When I see I'm being followed at a distance, I'll run over to the next aisle and wait till they catch up. Then I'll backtrack.

One time, after I got what I wanted, I went over to the store dick and told him that while he was busy watching me, someone could be stealing stuff. This was at Whole Foods in London.

I'm used to the clerks studying my credit card, but once, in Saks, I asked the clerk if he needed a magnifying glass, since he was taking so long, looking at it.

STAYING IN HOTELS...

I have had the hotel dicks following me when I've gone to my room. I get on the elevator and they step in and wait for me to push the button to my floor. Then, they get off, and watch me.

Happened in Cuba. Two nights in a row, as I entered, I was asked if I belonged there. I watched, and they were not asking the non-blacks.

Same thing in Puerto Rico at the pool, I was asked if I were a guest. Not the white guys with me.

TRAVELING...

Of course, I can't leave out US and UK Customs and Immigration. Oh, and Montenegro!

Two or three times, as I'm waiting in the priority line to board a plane, I've had people ask me to let them past, because they were priority – as if I wasn't. Two of those times, they were not even up front. Once, a man reminded me that the line we were in at security was for priority passengers only.

CRUISING...

One day, as I was coming out of my cabin, a man started telling me what he needed done in his cabin. Mind you, I had on my bb cap, shorts, and certainly was not dressed the way the cabin attendants were. He only saw one thing!

But alas, I'm not alone in this. I know a guy, Daum. We meet up on ships from time to time. He is of Filipino/Hispanic/Asian/Spanish ethnicity. He gets it all the time.

POLICED...

I had my famous racist run-in with the Metropolitan Police in London. I wanted to take it further, but my bestie in NY and Roger begged me not to, as I was going for my residency in the UK. I acquiesced. Not happily, but I did.

PERFORMING...

The last show I did was at a military base in England. It was a Christmas party on the base. I had a great time with them. I was told who the boss, commander, chief, captain, was (I'm not sure which branch I was working for) and they wanted me to have fun and pick on him. A good time was had by all.

When the show was over, the officer who hired me pulled me aside and asked if she could tell me something a little delicate. Sure. Of course. She wanted me to know that the booking agent had asked her if it was ok that I was a **coloured** guy. 2010!!! I was incensed. I was preparing to go all out on that woman who owned the agency, the next day. Roger calmed me and asked me not to. I didn't. SIGH. Anything to make him happy, I suppose.

LIVING...

There are many other occurrences and situations. I got used to the "What is *he* doing here? He can't belong here!" looks, long ago. As I explain to people, even if this profiling is not every day, I still keep that suit of armour at the door and put it on before I leave home, so I am prepared for what may come. It is a tough way to live, but one must live.

You *could* wonder why some people have an attitude.

I have rationalized that if it can happen to Oprah, as she has spoken about several times, I'm in good company.

AND STILL I RISE
1982

There is really nothing I can say or add to this, that most of us have not already been through and had to deal with.

I stopped counting when the number of people I knew who had died from AIDS hit 300, for me. And I think that was early 1990s. My brother Glenn, other relatives, my friend Glenn. Just about everyone in my circle of close friends. A sad fact of traveling around the world was that I knew people from everywhere. I miss them all, to this day, as I know we all do.

Give me stairs to the audience and I'm happy. Town Hall, NYC. 1973.

Aww, that smile.

The boy from Brooklyn.

I can never be serious. Laughing all the time.

Women ask me how I walk in them. I wonder myself sometimes.

I love this photo. Me in action.

Glenn singing with me in my show

Love those hands

I always wear red on television. Red draws your eye.

Cardiff Castle in Wales for Pride.

Tina with Grace Jones. Tina is wearing my fan club button.

Happy Halloween.

I want those cheekbones back again. SIGH.

Lily Savage. First performer I worked with in the UK. Great fun.

Look at that leg. Now I'm happy if I can lift it to get into my trousers. SIGH

I guess they like me sometimes.

Me and Mary Louise who was in Pearl's cast of Hello Dolly on Broadway.

I love how contemplative I am here

Anne Robinson after the taping of Weakest Link the second time.

Me and Kathy as church ladies doing a number in a show.

*I had this photo framed for my mom. She could see
her sonny boy dressed for a change.*

Me as Tina. That hair is heavy.

Playing a crazy person for a tv show.

ACT III

ROGER 1993

We met through an ad he placed in *Time Out* magazine. I was reading it on the way home from London to New York. I wasn't even looking for a boyfriend at the time. And especially not one 3,000 miles away. I figured maybe a half hour away was ideal. That gives one enough time to throw everything under the bed and jump in the shower when he says he's on his way over. But no – 3,000 miles!

This is the truth. As I read his ad, I said, "This one is mine." I really did.

He responded to my letter. We wrote back and forth for the next three months, until I returned to England. We met, and the rest is history.

Roger was extremely smart. And a very funny man. One time, he had me laughing so hard I could not catch my breath and I started to panic a bit. He had a kind heart (unlike someone we all know and love). Some said he had a calming effect on me. I called him "my fantasy man". We were perfectly suited. I saw the big picture, and Roger was great with the minutiae.

He was a scientist. Good with numbers. He took early retirement, realizing he couldn't work and hang out with me, too. In the beginning, we oscillated between the US and UK for the first couple of years together. I introduced him to cruising and our world changed. He loved it. We were always on the water, it seemed. I heard someone say, once, "Work is what I do between cruises." Yes. That is what we did. Cruise. Travel. Fly. Go to New York, do laundry, sleep, and off to another ship. Get back to England, do laundry, sleep. I might throw in a job, and then, off to another ship or plane. We were living the good life.

FOOD, GLORIOUS FOOD.

"You'd be good for this, Bryan," Roger said to me. He was reading our weekly local rag.

"What?"

"They're looking for food tasters."

"Whatever it is – yes! I'll do it." I wasn't looking for a job, but – food? I'm game.

Nestles, the chocolate company, was looking for part-time people to train to become sensory experts. Basically, food tasters for cereal. I responded to the ad.

I received a phone from the agency, asking me questions. I passed that bit, and would I come in for an interview?

"Yep."

One of the interesting parts of the interview was a test for colour blindness. It seems that males tend to have a much higher level of it than women. Who knew? I did the written parts, answered questions; then, they thanked me and I went home.

Several days later, the phone rang, "Hello, Bryan?"

"Yes."

"Are you excited?" the lady asked me.

"About what?"

"The job?"

"What job?" I'm puzzled now, 'cause I certainly wasn't looking for a job.

"With Nestles! We sent you a letter."

I never received it, but she gave me details – when to come in for orientation. The work would be three days a week and four hours a day. I figured, oh, why not? See what it's like, and if I'm not happy, I'm gone.

The training period was interesting. I would be working on the cereal products. Learning the different grains, textures, colours and shades of colours. The aromas of the products. I'll tell you, the shading was the most difficult part. Let's take the colour red. Ten different shades, and I'd have to put them in order of degrees of redness. With the training, I learned I am sensitive to salt. I have never liked salt, but never thought it would come in handy. I could usually find the salt in a product I tested.

Then, came the fun part. CAN YOU SAY 'CHOCOLATE'? Often, we got to work with chocolate. YES! And bring it home. And there was a company store, too, selling various Nestle items. Can you say 'discount'?

I worked there for just about two years, which was the longest time I've ever had a job. It was 11 women and me. They would talk about their men, as would I. I learned quite a bit about how some women think, and about what. If I had an out-of-town gig, or Roger and I went away, I was able to schedule time off with Nestles.

When I got a part in a play, it was time for me to say good-bye to my ladies and the job. It had been a grand time. I made friends. One lady, Sandy, was a witness for Roger and me when we got hitched. Another one, Belinda – we were always laughing. We said if we were in the same class, the teacher would have had to sit us at opposite ends of the room.

This was all new to me. Working. I'd never had an office Christmas party. Coffee breaks were never part of my working life. Vacation pay! Really? Wow. It was fun. Oh, and did I mention the chocolate?

ASSUME THE POSITION

Again, with our local newspaper. Roger was reading and came across a piece asking for people to volunteer to help the local constabulary. I don't recall the actual wording, but it was acting various roles to help train the new recruits. My honey said this was right up my alley. I called and set up an appointment to go in and speak with the police trainers. This was exciting and interesting.

They liked me and offered me the position. I'd be playing out various scenarios: the husband who beat his wife, thief who stole from a store, burglar or animal rights activist and other roles. I would go in and the instructors would give me the breakdown of what I was to say and play out. It got to the point where they would just tell me to play it by ear as I was interviewed by the students. I did the crime, or I didn't. No more instructions. "Just go for it, Bryan." I was thinking on my feet.

One day, one of the instructors asked if I wanted to try a new scene. It wouldn't be pleasant, but only if I was willing. Well, he had me with *It wouldn't be pleasant*. I was to accuse the officer of being a racist. He was from South Africa. Talk about drawing blood. I went all in, with guns blazing.

He did well. During the debriefing, the officer said he fell apart inside, but did what he was supposed to do. I got to play that out another time with another student, and this one could not cope. He melted. I apologized, but he was too far gone. He took it personally. The instructors always told the students, "No matter what Bryan does in here, it will be a million times worse when you get out on the beat."

For example, I heard of cases where an officer of the 'wrong' hue would not be allowed into a home. Same with female officers. Can you believe that? An officer is there to help you, and you refuse that help because of stupid shit?

Speaking of female officers, I came to this conclusion, and a trainer agreed with me. I found, in general, that females were better at defusing a situation than males. With men, it was testosterone at ten paces.

Later on, I had two officers tell me that they will never forget what they learned from me during training, because it will save their lives. That was thanks, for me. I am good at what I do.

I had noticed that they would bring in various people to talk about diversity. One might be gay, or a person of colour, a foreigner or drag queen. I said to Roger, "I want to do the diversity training. I am *all* of that and more."

I approached one the bosses and said I could talk about diversity, due to my background and they could eliminate employing several speakers by using just me. I was given the chance.

I put together a half-hour talk. My approach was different to how I had seen the other speakers operate. I turned it into a performance of sorts. I loved that. After class, sometimes a student would pull me aside to ask me questions or tell me about something in his or her personal life they were dealing with. I lived for that.

Whenever I went to the job, I had to call upstairs to have someone come down and let me in. Very annoying. I told Roger, "I'm going to get my warrant card" – which would open that damn door. I had no idea how that was going to happen, and I didn't care – but I wanted it. Well, need I tell you? I got it.

Occasionally, I would hear about other situations the police needed people for. One of them was visiting detainees to check on their welfare. Did they need anything? Had they eaten? Did they want to let someone know where they were? That type of thing.

I was attached to a great guy, who trained me to read the custody reports, what to say to the people who were in the cells and how to act with them. What *not* to say to them. If I felt in any danger, or if someone kicked off, there were alarm strips along the walls and I was to press them and stand back! Luckily, I never had any problem. I will say, the busiest time was Sunday mornings. People who were picked up after a night of drinking.

To do this job, I had to be interviewed at the county hall. I went in and answered their questions honestly as to why I wanted to do this. I think my response of wanting to give back to my adopted country sealed it for me.

Two weeks later, I was accepted and had to go to police headquarters to be photographed for my *warrant card*. I said to my honey, "I told you. I wanted one and got it." With this card, I was able to open the doors to four police buildings. YES!

For the six years I did this, I loved every second of it. But when I moved from Hertfordshire to Wimbledon, that ended my participation, sadly. One of the requirements for being part of this program was that you had to live in the county. I looked into seeing if I could do this with the Metropolitan Police of London (the Met). However, in spite of glowing letters from the Hertfordshire Constabulary, it was a "No. The Met has its own rules." Fair enough. Grrrrrrrr.

A benefit of doing all this was that it helped me to hone my acting craft, by thinking fast and learning to observe things. This came in handy when I did the tv show, *The People's Court*. It was with the fantastic performer and friend, Dave Lynn, with whom I adore working. It was filmed over two days. The second day was live, and just as they were about to start, I said, "That chair was not there yesterday." It looked out of place, to my eye. Everything stopped as the crew went back to check to see if I was correct. Ten minutes later – yes, Bryan was right.

By the by, Dave Lynn has asked me a couple of times to do one last show with him. That is so very kind of him; however, I don't think it will happen again. As I say to him, "I don't have Roger to zip me up."

I find it fun to watch a tv police show and say, "No, that's not right." Or "They can't do that." Knowledge is power – or it can spoil a show for you.

The one sad thing for me was to see the budget cutbacks for the police. Shameful and sad.

OLD AGE

I found this one on my own, without Roger this time. One day, at the doctor's office, on the bulletin board, there was a sign asking for people of a certain age to volunteer for a study on dementia. I said, why not? I got in touch with them and filled out a long survey about my life. They rang me and asked me to come in for a meeting.

The study is to find out why people are beginning to show signs of dementia at much younger ages, now. This study was to follow people and research lifestyle, medical and family history and anything else they could ascertain. Would I be interested in helping? Sure, why not?

I did a half-hour test of various types of questions. Written, verbal, and even had to do a drawing. My favourite was when she said count backwards from 100 by 7. Yeah, right.

When the test was over, I then had to speak to a therapist. I had him laughing non-stop. I told him that with my memory, if I ever did develop dementia, it would take ages to notice, because it would make me seem normal. My long and short term memories were as sharp as a Ginsu knife.

I could rattle off the dates, planes, trains, boats, and hotel schedule for the coming year.

People have asked me how I remember things, and I reply, "Don't know. I just do." I can recall things back to age three. Every teacher I ever had, up to college. The number of the hotel suite I was in, two weeks ago. My friends never buy the excuse that I've forgotten something, and if they ever decide to write a book, they will come to me and ask me what they did, and when.

I didn't qualify in what they were looking for and it ended up that they will use me as a control and check in with me three or four times a year to see how I'm doing.

Maybe that is why it was difficult writing this, because I can recall a lot. Now, what was I saying? I forget!

DREAMS. DREAMS ARE CHEAP. COST NOTHING. FREE. SO, DREAM.

I don't recall why or what it was about, but I heard on the radio that Elizabeth Taylor was a dual national: she had two passports. I said, "I want two passports." If I had to, I'd guess I was in my twenties. I already had been to Europe and had my one passport.

Fast-forward twenty-some years. I meet Roger. We start getting serious. Now, how can this work? We can't just keep going back and forth. OH, YEAH?

The Prime Mister, Tony Blair, as soon as he gets into

office, announced that same sex couples could apply for residency to be together. Ok. Now, there is hope for us.

We go to meetings of Stonewall, the gay organization that helps same sex couples. We talk with Lanis Levy, a lawyer who lives in the UK and is from Brooklyn! Assemble all the paperwork needed. We apply at the British Embassy in New York on a Friday. We show up with a large box of proof of the relationship. The man says, "Let's see what is in that magic box you have, there."

He was overwhelmed by what we had. My residency was granted the following week.

Now, no more third degree when I come into the UK at immigration. I have that stamp in my passport that opens doors.

Onward and upwards for us.

WE SHOULD BE DATING BY NOW

Now that I was allowed to live in the UK, time to get various legal things. Driver's license. In the UK, getting a license is not easy. I think almost everyone takes several hours of driver's ed. And I wonder why? From what I hear, a large number fail it the first time. I took two lessons and then the test. Fail. Not too badly, but fail.

There are two parts to it. Written, which I seem to recall is very long. Then, the practical. The tester and I are together forty minutes. I've never been in a car that long with someone unless he was taking me to dinner and then, dancing. When I got my Florida license, it took longer to walk to the car than the time we were in the car. The written test for driving in New York was honestly a joke. I looked at the book once, perhaps twice.

Each time I went back for the test, they had added more to it. One bit was called *show me, tell me*. The examiner asked me to show him and tell him how I fill up some tank under the hood. I said, "Oh honey, I get out the car and call people to come an' fix it." Amazingly, that is the time I did pass.

So, now I am legal to be on the roads. Not good, really. For those of us who are used to driving on the RIGHT side of the road, when we turn, we have a tendency to hit the left side of the curb. And there is no need to discuss roundabouts. Like in the Chevy Chase movie, European Vacation, we get into one and go round and round for hours. Glenn made it easy for me. He said, "Think of it as a yield sign." Got it. Never had trouble with one again. Thank you, Glenn.

OK. NEXT

After I put in my time, I can now apply for my citizenship. I can be a *dual*. I can have two passports.

My same Brooklyn-born British lawyer aids me towards becoming British. Documents of the last several years, my US passport and other things on hand. I sent them in on my birthday.

The following week, I get an envelope and I panic. Oh gee, I must have forgotten something to send in it. They are not happy. I have been turned down. I waited to open it, till Roger got home from the gym.

DAMN. ACCEPTED. Lanis said they were jumping up and down in the office. The turn-around was done quickly.

Now, came the ceremony thing. I could do a date with a group of others or pay to do it privately. I don't do groups. Private, please. The day of my swearing in, I had a cold and was not in a great mood. We arrived at the county hall early. I said to the lady as I tapped my wrist, "The car is on a meter. TICK, TOCK. TICK TOCK." To celebrate, we went to Costco for my chicken bake celebratory lunch. Yea.

I am now a British Citizen. Suck on that, Elizabeth Taylor. No more standing in the 'foreigner' lines at the airports in Europe. Dreams are free.

From my point of view, my elocution hasn't changed, but a number of times, folks in the states have said it has. I don't hear it, but I don't have to listen to myself.

COMMAND PERFORMANCE

I started reading about the marriages between gay guys, once the New York Times on Sunday started printing them. That was part of our Sunday routine when we were in the New York apartment. Get up, Sunday morning. Listen to the quiz on NPR radio, then go for breakfast, get the paper, go shopping, back home, then me and the Times. It was my dream to be listed there, one day. I loved reading about who proposed to whom, and how, and where, and all the details.

Probably from the time we began as a serious couple (I have no idea what that meant, or what began the process, or when it happened), I started asking Roger to marry me. I'd say it about 5 times a week. His response was always, "We can't. We're two men."

Oh yeah?

When it became legal to marry in the UK, that was it, for me. We talked about it briefly. I was ready. I wanted Roger legally. I wanted that piece of paper. Little did I ever think how important it would be, later on. After Roger died and I was trying to get all the legal stuff dealt with, my lawyer in New York said, "Thank goodness you have that marriage certificate, otherwise your life would be hell."

We were on a cruise around South America for the Xmas holidays. Now, I'm thinking with my American mind – people propose on a holiday. Christmas, birthday, New Years, Valentine's day, etc. I was thinking, ok, he'll do it during the holidays. I was looking for the ring in my food. Eating slowly, in case he put it in the dessert, or in something I could not see through. I only ordered foods you could see clearly through. I only drank water, so it would be easy to see the ring in the glass. At night, I'd check under my pillow. Look through everything before I put my clothes on. I was looking for that ring. I'd watch him closely in case he was acting out of sorts. Any unusual behavior.

Christmas eve. Christmas day. Boxing day (he is British, after all). New Year's Eve. New Year's day. Nothing. Nada. No ring. Not a hint. Zilch.

So, I'm thinking – my birthday. That's it. He's waiting for my birthday. He knows how important my birthday is to me. And in my mind, to the rest of the international world. That's when he will pull out the ring and pop the question.

All birthday, not a thing. That night. Ok, this is it. It's now. My birthday is almost over. It will happen now. Nope.

The next morning, I woke up and said to myself, I am not waiting for Valentine's day, if that is what he has in mind. I said, "Honey, sit down. We have to talk!"

I always thought I asked him. He said, no – I *told* him we were getting married. It was not a question of "Will you – ?" It was a command.

I didn't care. I was marrying my honey.

HERE COMES THE...GROOMS

Ok. Now, we needed to work on a wedding. Two good things about Roger and I. He was *teeny-tiny* detail orientated. He was "Do big A, section number 1; then 1.1; then subset 1.1.a. etc., then go on to the big B." That was the scientist in him. I was A to Z in one second, don't pass go and don't collect $200! That was the BRYAN in me.

We were coming back from our trip and I was going

straight into rehearsal for a play. I figured it would be fun to get married on stage after the play closed. In the U.S., you can get married anywhere. In the supermarket, underwater, while sky-diving. Any place the two people agree on and can get the officiate to say yes to. Not in the UK. It was church or the town registry office. What do I know? I'm a Yank. Things have loosened up, since then.

I'd say 90% of the work was done by Roger. I'd come home from the play and he'd tell me what he had achieved during the day. He did a great job of it. It was the registry office, for us. I planned it for March 23, Roger's birthday. This way, he could never forget the date.

I can stand in front of a few thousand people and not think a thing of it. Here I was, in front of thirty friends and family, and my knees were knocking. On the video, you can see my hands moving 90 miles a second. Mr *I'm a shy person and don't like to be out front* was as calm as if he'd done this a thousand times and it was no big deal. Ahh, my honey. Luckily, I have the video, since I don't recall the ceremony.

The both of us wanted something nice, fast, over and done. We chose a fantastic centuries-old restaurant for the reception. People from both families came. It was a wonderful day.

I DO. I DO. AGAIN

I subscribe to several gay news sites. I read that the Governor of the state of Massachusetts had signed a law that same sex couples would be allowed to get married there. Silly Roger said, "Since we're docking there on a cruise, perhaps we should get married there, too."

He told me he only said that as a joke. You'd think, after over ten years, the man would have known me by then. I did not take it as a joke. I loved the idea.

Bryan put his thinking cap on and went to work on it. Again, long story short. We got married on the dock, with the ship in the background of the photo. My friend, Thom, was ordained for the day, to be able to marry us. We were now married in/on two continents. I'm no dummy. Roger was going to have to go to Asia to get rid of me. I knew what I was doing. I had the man of my dreams, worldwide.

As an aside – talking about "you'd think he knew me by now," we were in Brussels, which is known for lace and chocolate. I was not looking for doilies, that is for sure. I buy a big bag of chocolate and start chowing down. My cutie says he thought I bought the candy to take home!!!!! What? I said it would be amazing if the chocolate made it back to the ship, and even more amazing if he got more than one piece! He could be so cute, sometimes. *To take home,* indeed!

THANK GOODNESS FOR ROGER

No matter how many people I lost over the years, and however they died, I went on. Part of life, they say. Well, losing my mom was devastating to me. The last two years of her life, she hadn't been well. We're talking a lady who did not believe in being sick.

Mom did not need 24-hour care. She did have a carer for twelve hours a day. They got along well, and people assumed they were mother and daughter. Azalia was a great help for us. She enabled me to be away from home.

I got home to New York four days before mom had a stroke. Roger had come in the day before. He was where he needed to be. With me. For a week, it was back and forth with us and the hospital. Mom's best friend, Marie, whom I had known all my life, talked and explained things to me. She had been a head nurse before she retired.

The doctors said there was only 10% of brain function. I was holding onto that 10%. Miss Marie assured me of what I already knew in my heart, that mom would have hated this. Mom and I had spoken of these things before. A comment on something in the news media, perhaps. We could not understand how people could be hooked up to machines for years. She felt it was cruel. Quality of life, was her thought. We don't let animals suffer, so why humans? For eighty-two years, she had been an active person. Running here and there. Doing this. Doing that.

In the 60s, fashion changed. Women weren't dressing up and wearing hats and gloves. Cotillions were few and far between, and mom went back to school, got her master's degree and taught school where she had attended as a child. I have her degrees on my wall, now. Even with Azalia, she kept on the move as much as she was able.

I met the hospital board, with Roger and Miss. Marie supporting me. It was decided that mom would be disconnected from life support. Most difficult thing I had ever done, but it was the right thing.

I don't know how I would have made it through, without Roger. He was what I needed. He took good care of me. When I think about losing my guardian angel, I think how fortunate I was to have had my mom for forty-nine years. Guiding, caring, loving me. As my grief counsellor said, I light up when I speak of my mom. She was good.

NEEDLESS TO SAY, BRYAN IS NOT TAKING THIS LYING DOWN

Roger started feeling ill, late 2010. I knew there was a problem when we were on a ship and he took the elevator a few times. He always took the stairs and made me, also. The doctor thought perhaps it was food-related. I started to cook different things. Bland, soft, nothing foreign. Meds for his stomach. Still not better.

We continued to travel around the globe. Roger was careful as to what he ate. One trip we did to the Middle East, I tried to convince him to forego the trip and stay home and go to the doctor. Nope. He wasn't having it.

We were home in New York, and I suppose he had had enough. We made an appointment for as soon as we got back to England, the following week.

June 6, 2011. I won't forget it. That began seven months of hell. Tests and tests and more tests. Overnight hospital stays. Weekly visits to hospitals and clinics. Back and forth. Finally, a cause. Mesothelioma is difficult to confirm, and it took several weeks of tests to get a confirmation. Once Roger was officially diagnosed, he waited to tell people.

He sent out an email explaining what he had been dealing with. Roger thanked everyone for their concern and ended it with: "NEEDLESS TO SAY, BRYAN IS NOT TAKING THIS LYING DOWN."

And he was correct about that. I got books, researched online, spoke to anyone I could. I wanted to be prepared for the fight of *my* life. Never mind Roger's. The gloves were off.

There was never a moment when I thought I'd be giving up. I was determined. I did tell Roger that if he ever said to me, "Enough," I'd quit. But until then, it was man the battle stations. He never did, and I never did, until his last night.

When we had no appointments and some spare time, Roger and I had some amazing talks. Roger said we should have known something was coming down the pike. Everything was just going great. We did things as if we had to cram things in. Looking back, it did appear that he was correct. If it were possible, we became even closer, the last two or three years. I love my work. Love it. LOVE IT. However, I do see that I was only giving it ninety-eight per cent, those years. My time with Roger was sacrosanct. I am sure I could have had more of a career, but Roger came first. I was never into playing the game. Not my scene. My relationship was much more important to me.

Being Roger, he planned my life for me. My future life without him. Down to a different vacuum cleaner. He thought of everything, I believe. He had to cajole and force me to participate and pay attention, though. I did not want to deal with it. He gave me great advice.

We had already gone over whether I planned to stay in the UK or return to New York. My decision was stay in the UK, since that is where our lives had been. Then, where would I live? Without even bring it up, he knew I was not going to live in the house without him. We lived in a quiet cul-de-sac, in a market town called Hitchin, thirty miles north of London. One day, I said to Roger, "Listen to that!"

He said, "What? I don't hear anything."

"Exactly!"

He suggested moving to London, near our friends, Stuart and Furdoon. He felt they would be the best ones to help me adjust. Sure enough, he was right. They found me this great place. There is life here. I hear police cars screaming down the street at 2 A.M. Fire trucks and ambulance sirens and car alarms going off. *"Children of the night. What music they make,"* to quote Dracula. I'm home.

Something that Roger said sticks in my memory. During one of our many heavy conversations, he said he was glad it was the way it was. He knew I would be fine, at some point. Had the circumstances been different, he wasn't sure how he would do.

He said to go on a cruise and spread his ashes on the water. For his birthday, two months after he died, I put some of his ashes in the Nile. We had always said we'd do the Nile, but something else always came up. Roger's ashes are in waters around the world. Atlantic, Pacific, Indian, North Sea, Caribbean, and English Channel.

A visiting nurse suggested he register with a hospice near us. You could go in for a day and relax. Take health and wellness therapies. See medical people. All sorts of things. Being a Yank, I suggested getting professional therapy. We had different therapists. I was told couples are always concerned about the other person, and not themselves. I couldn't argue with that.

The people at Garden House Hospice we more than gold, platinum, manna from heaven. Their kindness and love was beyond. They were great. Well…! Roger was in the hospice for twelve days. I would go in and out a few times a day. Soon, the people on the front desk knew me and I'd smile and walk in. One – and I'm going to be nice about her here – complained.

One of the nurses said to me, "Bryan, just stop and say who you are, and that will make her happy, she is just that way."

I said, no problem. Of course.

The next time I went in and she was there, I stopped, smiled and said, "Hello. I'm Bryan Murphy. I'm here to see my **husband**, Roger Gibbens."

She called and said, "Mr. Murphy is here to see his **partner**, Roger Gibbens. Shall I send him back now?"

In a nanosecond, a thousand scenarios went through my mind for how to deal with that slight. And in none of them did she end off well. Her life flashed before my eyes. I will say that sweet and kind Roger in one ear won out, over the boy from Brooklyn in the other ear. I let it go. I sucked it up. I'M STILL FUCKING HOT ABOUT THAT. Not that she said what she did, but the fact that I let it go. I ate it. I did not say anything. A valuable lesson for me. As a friend once said to me, sometimes a rolled-up newspaper is better to hit a fly than a bazooka. Perhaps, but I like bazookas.

I sat and slept in the chair next to his bed. I was offered a bed in another room. I thanked them and said no. "I'll stay in the chair." My thoughts were, "I'll be in this chair for however long it takes for him to get better." I would run home, do quick stuff and rush back to him.

Roger hadn't spoken for a day or so, and the day before he died, he said "Bryan". I jumped up. He pointed to his mouth to alert me that he felt it was dry. The nurse had given me a small water holder and I sprayed his mouth. The thought that I might have missed him calling for me still upsets me. He said "Bryan" and he knew Bryan was there. That was all that mattered.

Around three in the morning, the nurses came in to tend to him. I stood outside. If I'm ever offered a bazillion dollars, I'll never be able to explain the following.

I heard a voice say to me, "He's not going to get better, Bryan. Go home."

The nurses finished their duties. I went back in, collected my things, and this is what I call my Brokeback Mountain moment – just as in the film, I took his coat. I have no idea why. There were other belongings of his, but I took his coat!

Kissed him, said, "I will always love you. Thank you for everything." And I left.

The nurse asked if I were ok. I said, "No, but I will be."

She let me out the side door into a cold, foggy January morning. I sat in the car crying for a while, then I drove home and fell across the bed at 4:20 AM. The hospice rang me four hours later.

Sunday, January 29, 2012, I lost my fight against cancer. Roger died. I was a widower.

Seven billion people in the world, and for the first time in sixty-two years, I was alone. Totally alone. By myself. I had no one.

I went into executive mode.

This was difficult to write.

The first time we got Hitched. England. 2006.

The second time we got hitched. On the dock in Boston, USA. 2008.

Roger always made me laugh.

After a gig in Palm Springs. Roger is so handsome. I loved him in a tux.

Iceland. He said it was MY idea to rent bikes. I still don't believe it.

Me and my cutie. This is my favorite picture of us.

CURTAIN

ENCORE

WE HAD FACES, THEN

When I did my first set of professional photos, way back when, I showed them to a casting agent. She said I had a rubber face. A *what?* Some actors were not able to do facial reactions. I was able to change my facial reactions in each photo – and that was good. That meant nothing to me, at the time.

I went to a casting for a movie. I would be playing in a scene with Susannah York. The casting agent and I role-played several scenarios, which were filmed. He seemed pleased with what I did. Heard that before – but ok, fine.

Ed, my agent, sent an email saying he'd received a note from the casting people. They loved what I did. Loved it. But – there is always a but! – I filmed too young for what they were looking for. I was seen due to my playing age, but on camera, my "*youthful*" face betrayed me. I guess I could take that as a compliment. An actor friend reassured me that it is unusual for casting folk to take the time to send a note such as that to an agent. Wow. I must have really impressed them.

In an acting class, the instructor told us to bring in our professional photos and we would critique them. When mine was put on screen... Ready? They put my age as twenty years younger than my real age. I hear some of you! SHUT UP!

I told Roger that, in general, with us black folk, as long as the person is healthy, whatever age you think they are, you can usually add a good ten years or more.

Fast-forward, fifty years later. My agent calls and says, "Go to a casting for a commercial."

I jump up and out the door. The men wanted to see my facial reactions to different scenarios. They would say, "Surprised!" and I'd look surprised. Tell me to look shocked. I gave them shocked. And on, and on. Each time, they would look at each other and say, "Yes, he's good," and smile. "Yes, that's what we want."

Yeah, right. I know that routine. I did what they asked, they thanked me, and I walked out the door for home.

Agent Ed calls later and tells me they liked what I did, and I got the job. Yes. All because of my rubber face. I played a pharmacist and had to facially react to a customer.

I hadn't worked since Roger got sick and it is sort of ironic that I started my career with my rubber face and ended it with my rubber face. This was my last gig.

SWIPE LEFT, SWIPE RIGHT, FACE NORTH, JUMP UP, JUMP DOWN, TURN AROUND, PICK A BALE OF COTTON.

'm a dinosaur. Old fashioned. Out of my depth here, when it comes to dating. "What? Dating, you say, Bryan? Do tell us more."

Hold your horses. Quite a number of friends are going to be happy to hear this.

Once I'd stopped playing the poor, sad, lonely, bitter, old widower sympathy card when necessary, and after being single for a number of years, and still reading the Sunday New York Times wedding section online, I thought, Oh Bryan, what have you got to lose? I was hearing about more and more people meeting online. Swiping in all directions, north, south, whichever. No, not my thing.

I noticed that most couples met through the site OkCupid, so I thought a dating site might be better. More like the old days. Chatting first, calling, getting to know each other a bit before meeting. YES, I PLACED AN AD. Ok, people? I did. I placed an ad in/on OK CUPID.

A couple of days go by, and I got a hit, I guess you call

it. His name was John. I hear Roger right now: "Brevity, Bryan. Brevity. The truncated version, Bryan."

OK!!! So, six years after losing Roger and 25 years after my last date, which *was* Roger, I had a date with a gentleman. We met and went to a nice romantic sort of coffee, cake, light snacks restaurant by the Old Vic theater.

I arrived first, and may I tell you, from the moment he said hello to the second we said good-bye, he did everything – EVERYTHING right. The two desserts, one plate, two forks, talking, jokes, looks. He restored my faith in love, life, dating. And John had an Irish accent that could melt butter. I could have listened to him read the phone book. Besides him being great-looking, it was the accent. That accent! Couple of red flags, but no matter – it was the date. It was perfect.

I was going away, as usual. He was going away. "We'll catch up, upon our returns." A couple of emails during our trips, and that was it. He did not respond. It was ok. My first date had been perfect. PERFECT. That was the important thing, to me.

A month or two go by, and another hit that piqued my interest. A NOO YAWKER. I said to myself, Oh great, a NOO YAWKER and I'm no longer there. But no matter. Roger lived 3,000 miles away. Plus, this guy, also called John, sent a photo taken in an airport lounge. He traveled. Good start. I Googled him and he was true to his word: Harvard. Yes, I said HARVARD. Wow. He was an interesting man. We shared several interests.

"BREVITY, BRYAN!"

OK ROGER!

We met for brunch at probably my favourite restaurant in Florida. HUH? I flew in from England, he flew in from New York. It just worked out that way. We were coming in the same day.

Good date. Not great. But it was good. And that was, once again, reassuring me about my dating future. One or two red flags. We did calls and emails, and that was it. Ok. I was fine with it. It was the date, and helping me to feel good about getting back into the dating world. Little did I know what I was about to do.

FIRST DATES TV SHOW

And last date! – Boo hoo

I would watch the telly show, FIRST DATES, whenever there was a gay couple on. This was filmed in a restaurant in London. There was also the sister show to it, called FIRST DATES HOTEL. One time, I was watching, and at the end there was an announcement: "If you want to be on the show, here is how to enter."

I made a note of it. I was interested in the hotel show. Free hotel in some country. Oh yeah, right up my alley.

I looked over the requirements for the show. I vacillated – yes, no, yes, no. This was not my thing, to go on a show such as this. I asked a few people – would they dare? Not mentioning that I was thinking about doing it. Two weeks later, I hit 'send.'

Two things dawned on me *after* I hit send, of course. They probably only fly you coach, and I knew there was no way that was going to happen with me. However, I thought, Bryan, you are doing a personal ad for a few thousand guys. Why not, then? But still, I was not going to fly economy.

Someone from the show got in touch a few days later. The woman explained things to me. This was going to be for the restaurant show. Ok, getting better. That would be just a car service. She said it would be a 45-minute chat. Well, I took over, and we were done in thirty! I was told a producer would get back to me if they were interested. Producer calls a few days later. Again, we'd be chatting for a while. Over in fifteen minutes, and would I be willing to come in to talk and be filmed, so they could see how I do in front of the camera?

Me? Little ol' me? On camera? Talking? Ok. I don't know if I can do that, but I'll try.

As if!

I arrived, and when it was my time, they sat me in front of the camera. The producer began asking questions about me, my love life, my husband, the type of man I was looking for, goals, hobbies, etc. All the things one should ask on a first date, or no later than the second one.

I told them, "I won't date any man who has a waist smaller than the size of my thigh. I do love a dad bod on a man. Age-wise, I'm *barely* civil to a man who is in his lower 40s – and under that, he doesn't even exist in my world."

I did think of mentioning he should have a Black Amex, but I didn't. I thought it, though.

I took over the room and the filming lasted almost a half hour longer than they planned. I had them on the floor laughing. They thanked me for coming in and they would be getting back to me. As they were ushering me out the door, I still had the body mic on. They were so busy laughing, they forgot about it.

I was honest and told them it was going to be difficult to find a match for me. And come show night, I was right.

I had made three rules for myself:
1. Do not order any food that drips, leaks, spills, or splashes.
2. Remember his name.
3. And lastly, just have fun.

It was a fun evening. Lovely gentleman, but he was not what I was looking for, and I certainly wasn't his type. When I asked him the type of man he liked, he was kind and said, "The more *trimmed* type." He could have put it a whole lot of other not-so-nice ways.

What I think happened – we were the last show filmed

for the season, and they must have said, "Oh, just throw these two together."

Oh well, last date. That was 2018. Sigh.

HEALTH

Never mind gold, jewels, Rolex watch, money, house in Beverly Hills, body of a Greek god, all your own teeth. Nothing matters as much as health.

Growing up, we were not allowed to be sick: there wasn't any illness at nine A.M. and feeling better after three P.M. If we were sick on Friday and could not go to school, there was no Our Lady of *Anywhere* coming down and performing a miracle healing at three o'clock – we were sick the entire weekend. Not that we didn't try to pull that stunt from time to time; but somehow, mom always knew when it was real.

I developed arthritis in my knee at 10 years old – born with the gene, according to doctors. I recall running to school and falling, and then – boom – arthritis. It hurt. Just plain hurt. A lot.

Off to my G.P., Dr. Rosenberg. He must have been a hundred and fifty years old, then. He was old school. He told mom I was too young to be put on the new drug, cortisone. Let it hurt. I'll get used to it. If it's just too much, give me aspirin. And to this day, I thank him for that. It helped me to deal with pain. When I have an attack sometimes, I am aware of it, but keep on going.

I go all through life with that idea of dealing with illness, and along comes my honey, Roger – and if he didn't see blood or the bone sticking out of me, he wasn't buying my bout of man flu. He must have cross-referenced with my mom.

GOUT

I always knew I was upper class. Born to the purple. Was regal and royal. There was no doubt in my mind I was a blue blood. We were on a cruise – yes, I know, big surprise – and I woke up in agony. Pain as I'd never had before, I don't think. My arthritis was nothing, compared to this. I dragged myself to the ship's doctor, stuck my foot in his face and begged him, "Lay hands upon me. Heal me."

He took his thumb and put it close to my toe and I started yelling. He hadn't even touched me. Gout!

It was a defining moment, to me. That assured me. I had proof. I belonged to the aristocracy. Henry VIII, Alexander the Great, et al, also had it. They were my posse.

I said, "If I must be in pain, at least let it be a wealthy man's illness."

The doctor thought I was nuts. He explained what about it and why.

Roger said, "Or it could have been the six lobsters you had last night for dinner."

Thank you, Roger!

The doctor says gout is usually in the genes and if I do

have arthritis, it's all related, and the six lobsters caused the flare-up. I'm sure, on a ship, he sees this all the time, with all the food.

A shot, pills and in about an hour, I was much better. Roger got me a wheelchair and rolled me around the ship. I skipped lines. Went straight to the front. I played it for all it was worth.

Usually, the gout flares up about once a month. I have the pills now, in case I need them. Most of the time, I can tell when it's about ready to blow. I hobble for a day or so until the pills take effect. The only time it has caused me a problem is when I was in a show at the London Palladium, but trust me, I put on those heels and danced and sang across that stage. Anything for show biz. This was Judy's Palladium, after all. No way was I gonna mess that up.

I think this lockdown has prepared me for my dystopian health world. With the way I believe my arthritis is heading, in the not too distant future world, I'll be under permanent lockdown. But until then...!!!

I don't know how much longer I will be able to do much. Walking and standing can be problematic at times and it's in my hand now. I can feel it slowly moving over to my left hand. EEK. I have to be careful holding anything hot or sharp. I have no trouble holding a fork of course! Mind you, I am not complaining, just commenting. As always, I'm looking on the bright side. Unlike some folk who can find the downside to anything in a second, I'm not one of them.

We all know people who look for things to complain about so they can bitch. That is not me. I can't speak Esperanto and I can't be negative. Look how many years I was able to do what I wanted without thinking about the arthritis.

Those things and a few age-related aches and pains. Now every time you go to the doctor, or anything medical, it always starts with, "As one ages...!" Oh, well.

My mantra is, I do what I can, when I can, and as much as I can.

GRIEF

One of the positive things to have come out of the lockdown for me – if you want to call it positive – was grieving. Some friends had wondered, or asked, if I had dealt with Roger's death.

I'd say, "I take it one second (or minute, or hour, or day) at a time." That I was coming along "as well as could be expected."

Some even said that perhaps, with all my traveling, running non-stop, maybe I hadn't. Maybe my travel was really just me running away from the grief. I would say to them, "I'm good. I'm travelling – as Roger and I did. I'll be fine."

Well, may I tell you, I was wrong.

How I know I am grieving is – my emotions have been all over the place. Up, down, etc. The grief has knocked the hell out of me. All this time at home alone has been good for that. I've had to face losing Roger. I believed I had. Oh yeah, intellectually, yes – but not emotionally. I don't know if this will be it or not, but it has been cathartic for me.

Now, when I say one day at a time, I understand the meaning.

DONE

The most difficult thing about writing this book has been keeping it to myself and not telling anyone. But then again, that is why people tell me things. They know I will never, ever tell anyone else. See? I would make a great spy.

I've had a year and was just too lazy. I've been writing since first or second grade. I wrote a poem.

KITES

Kites fly,
fly so high,
they may someday
reach the sky.

How 'bout that? Many years ago, I wrote a book of poetry, and would read one or two poems in my shows. I spoke to a literary agent who liked the work, but said poetry doesn't sell unless you already have a name. Over the years, friends have asked me to write important letters for them. I've written for a number of magazines, both in the US and the UK.

I took a writing class a few years back. One assignment was to write a page length about something in the home and read it to the class and have them critique it. I wrote about me in the home after Roger died. I read it and stopped the room cold. Dead. Silence. After what seemed minutes, but probably several seconds, the instructor spoke up and asked me if it were true. I said yes. He sent me a note saying I was a talented writer. My writing was a breath of fresh air. I should continue to write.

Twenty years ago, I wrote a novel in thirty days. It was crap, by the way, but it was two hundred and something pages' worth and I did it. That had to be made up. This was my life, and it's taken forever.

I spend my days watching opera from Lincoln Center in New York. And armchair plane-spotting – London Heathrow. I could spend hours watching the planes coming and going.

I will say I am annoyed at myself, though. With the time off, I should have been speaking German fluently. Why? This goes back to my dementia study. I learned that as one ages, one should work on the brain and keep it active. I decided to learn a language. I am down with the romance languages, so I needed to learn some other type. I go to Germany a few times a year and thought it would help a bit for me to speak the language. I have a friend who is German and was helping me, but I think she has given up on me. I stand contrite.

Now, I can get back to my books and reading them. I have them stacked up, just waiting for me. I love to read. Always have. When I was in grade school, during the summer, the local library had a program for children to encourage them to read. If a child read ten books over the summer, he or she would receive an award. I earned mine easily.

When I travel, I am always reading. Flying is reading time for me. As much as I hate to admit it, I do like the Kindle. It's not easy to travel with ten books, but with the stupid machine, I have books at my fingertips. I held out as long as I could before I capitulated. I love holding a book. Smelling the paper. Turning the pages. But you can't stop progress.

As we come out of house arrest, I'll probably go back to the road again. My travel agent, Laura G. and I have been together almost 20 years. I'm sure she misses me but I don't think I'll be doing eight to ten months anymore. I've seen most of the world. A hundred and thirty-plus countries. So, not much more to do. They've taken away my A380 and 747 planes, which spoils a lot of flight-time for me. I can't go to any country with an anti-gay stance. That rules out Russia and Egypt, which are two of my favourite places to visit.

It has been an amazing time, being home. I have loved sleeping in my own bed. My bed knows where the lumps and bumps are. I wake up at night and know where the bathroom is. When Tina retired, she said she was looking forward to the quiet and wanted solitude. I get her, on that.

I have my classical music playing softly in the background most of the day. Not having to smile and talk to people before I've finished my coffee. My sweats have become de rigueur. I like to sit in the outdoor space of my fabulous apartment (thank you, Furdoon and Stuart) with my coffee, croissant and newspaper, and laugh at people doing the walk of shame on Sunday mornings. Such fun.

I am fortunate and am so fucking grateful. I have lived the life – including Roger. The life I planned and fantasied about as a kid. I didn't know how, but I knew. I KNEW!

Life is grand, ain't it?

BOWS

THANKS EVERYONE

CUE EXIT MUSIC
CURTAIN
HOUSE LIGHTS

BRYAN HAS LEFT THE BUILDING

My rubber face in my last job. I played a pharmacist.

He's so cool. My last photo before lockdown. Family wedding.

StoryTerrace

CPSIA information can be obtained
at www.ICGtesting.com
Printed in the USA
LVHW020743021121
702215LV00010B/295